SCIENCE BEHIND SPORTS

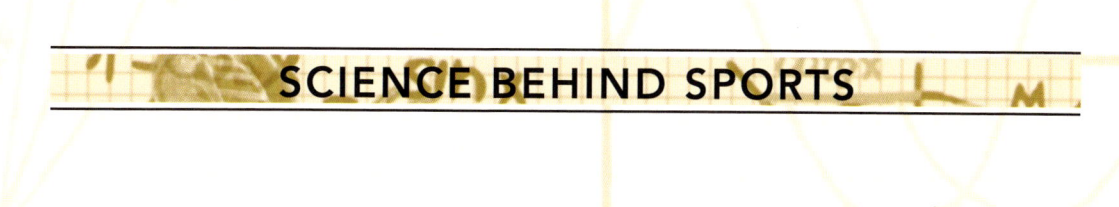

Track and Field

Other titles in the Science Behind Sports series:

Baseball
Basketball
Football
Gymnastics
Ice Hockey
Snowboarding
Soccer
Swimming

SCIENCE BEHIND SPORTS

Track and Field

JENNY MACKAY

LUCENT BOOKS
A part of Gale, Cengage Learning

**GALE
CENGAGE Learning**

Detroit • New York • San Francisco • New Haven, Conn • Waterville, Maine • London

GALE
CENGAGE Learning

© 2012 Gale, Cengage Learning

ALL RIGHTS RESERVED. No part of this work covered by the copyright herein may be reproduced, transmitted, stored, or used in any form or by any means graphic, electronic, or mechanical, including but not limited to photocopying, recording, scanning, digitizing, taping, Web distribution, information networks, or information storage and retrieval systems, except as permitted under Section 107 or 108 of the 1976 United States Copyright Act, without the prior written permission of the publisher.

Every effort has been made to trace the owners of copyrighted material.

LIBRARY OF CONGRESS CATALOGING-IN-PUBLICATION DATA

MacKay, Jenny, 1978-
  Track and field / by Jenny MacKay.
    p. cm. -- (The science behind sports)
  Includes bibliographical references and index.
  ISBN 978-1-4205-0707-2 (hardcover)
  1. Track and field--Juvenile literature. 2. Sports sciences. I. Title.
  GV1060.55.M24 2012
  796.42--dc23
                                                                    2011030511

Lucent Books
27500 Drake Rd
Farmington Hills MI 48331

ISBN-13: 978-1-4205-0707-2
ISBN-10: 1-4205-0707-9

Printed in the United States of America
1 2 3 4 5 6 7 15 14 13 12 11

TABLE OF CONTENTS

Foreword	6
Chapter 1 A Run Through Track-and-Field History	8
Chapter 2 The Race Is On: Sprints, Distance Races, and Hurdles	20
Chapter 3 Up, Up, and Away: Jumping Events and the Pole Vault	35
Chapter 4 A Toss-Up: Shot Put, Hammer Throw, Discus, and Javelin	48
Chapter 5 Staying on Track: Fitness and Injury Prevention	63
Chapter 6 Ninety Percent Mental: The Psychology of Track and Field	79
Notes	92
Glossary	95
For More Information	96
Index	99
Picture Credits	103
About the Author	104

FOREWORD

On March 21, 1970, Slovenian ski jumper Vinko Bogataj took a terrible fall while competing at the Ski-flying World Championships in Oberstdorf, West Germany. Bogataj's pinwheeling crash was caught on tape by an ABC *Wide World of Sports* film crew and eventually became synonymous with "the agony of defeat" in competitive sporting. While many viewers were transfixed by the severity of Bogataj's accident, most were not aware of the biomechanical and environmental elements behind the skier's fall—heavy snow and wind conditions that made the ramp too fast and Bogataj's inability to maintain his center of gravity and slow himself down. Bogataj's accident illustrates that, no matter how mentally and physically prepared an athlete may be, scientific principles—such as momentum, gravity, friction, and aerodynamics—always have an impact on performance.

Lucent Book's Science Behind Sports series explores these and many more scientific principles behind some of the most popular team and individual sports, including baseball, hockey, gymnastics, wrestling, swimming, and skiing. Each volume in the series focuses on one sport or group of related sports. The volumes open with a brief look at the featured sport's origins, history and changes, then move on to cover the biomechanics and physiology of playing, related health and medical concerns, and the causes and treatment of sports-related injuries.

In addition to learning about the arc behind a curve ball, the impact of centripetal force on a figure skater, or how water buoyancy helps swimmers, Science Behind Sports readers will also learn how exercise, training, warming up, and diet and nutrition directly relate to peak performance and enjoyment of the sport. Volumes may also cover why certain sports are popular, how sports function in the business world, and which hot sporting issues—sports doping and cheating, for example—are in the news.

Basic physical science concepts, such as acceleration, kinetics, torque, and velocity, are explained in an engaging and accessible manner. The full-color text is augmented by fact boxes, sidebars, photos, and detailed diagrams, charts and graphs. In addition, a subject-specific glossary, bibliography and index provide further tools for researching the sports and concepts discussed throughout Science Behind Sports.

CHAPTER **1**

A Run Through Track-and-Field History

Running, jumping, and throwing may be the oldest athletic activities in human history. Not only do they require little in the way of specialized equipment, as many modern sports like football or golf do, they are physical tasks that people instinctively know how to do. Humans have been running, jumping, and throwing since long before there were any formal contests of strength and speed. Long ago these were skills necessary to preserve life. How fast people ran or how high they could jump possibly determined whether they would become prey. How accurately and powerfully a hunter threw a stone or a spear may have been the difference between a successful hunt or going hungry. As groups of early humans banded together into tribes or clans, they also fought each other from time to time, so the fastest runners, most fleet-footed jumpers, and strongest spear throwers likely made excellent warriors as well.

Little is known about those early humans and their lifestyle, because most primitive groups of people had no system of writing with which to tell a permanent story about their way of life. Cave paintings and engravings from ancient times are rare and tell modern scientists little about how early humans lived and played. Athletic feats like running, jumping, and throwing may have been vital survival skills, but they probably were not sporting events that entertained cheering audiences. Much had to change in the world to make track and field the spectator sport that it is today.

Early Athletes and Their Fans

Eventually, humanity became more civilized. People who had once lived in clans or tribes began to form larger communities, and these grew into towns and then cities. The ancient Egyptians were one civilization known for the size of their cities and the ingenuity of their inventors. During the heyday of their civilization, from about 3000 B.C. to 500 B.C., ancient Egyptians built giant monuments such as the pyramids. They also developed a system of writing in pictures and symbols, which they used to chisel stories of their way of lifes into the stone surfaces of buildings and other artifacts that still remain today. From these stories and pictures, archaeologists—scientists who study human history from the objects people leave behind—have learned that the ancient Egyptians had

Archaeologists have restored this Sed festival courtyard, where events to demonstrate the pharaoh's athletic skills were held in ancient Egypt.

RUNNING YOUNG

70,000

Number of Americans ages seventeen and under who compete in USA Track & Field's annual Junior Olympics championships. Many athletes who make the official Olympic team start out as Junior Olympians.

gatherings where spectators could watch athletic feats. Among these events were Sed festivals, in which the pharaoh, or ruler of Egypt, performed to display his power. The pharaoh, considered almost godlike by his people, made a circuit on foot around posts or markers to display to the crowd how fast and strong he was. He had no competitors in these events, since it was unthinkable in ancient Egyptian culture for anyone to defeat the pharaoh at something. The festivals had great religious and social meaning to the Egyptians, but they also demonstrated that a person's running speed was considered important to Egyptian culture and that fast runners were admirable—a theme that developed in other advanced cultures of the ancient world, too.

The civilization that best represents the history of track-and-field events as we know them today is that of ancient Greece. The Greeks were fighters. By the year 1600 B.C., they had grown into a large, powerful society that ruled much of what is now Europe, mainly due to the strength of their military. Warriors were highly prized in ancient Greek culture, and soldiers trained for war by running and throwing things to build strength and speed. The Greeks had a very organized and highly developed society. They built grand cities ruled by sophisticated governments, and they had a great love for recreation, competition, and performance. The Greeks may have been the first culture to organize sporting events for the sole purpose of entertaining crowds. Modern archaeologists have found written records and painted artifacts like vases that indicate that footraces and throwing competitions were very popular in ancient Greek culture. At first, these competitive events took place during funerals and religious festivals as a way to honor gods that the Greeks worshipped. In the year 776 B.C., however, the Greeks held a new kind of sporting festival, organized especially for spectators—the first known track-and-field competition in history.

A Rock-Hard Body

In the fifth century B.C. a Greek sculptor named Myron created one of the most famous works of art in history—a bronze statue called *Discobolus,* or "the discus thrower." Although the original statue no longer exists, several copies were made in white marble that can still be seen in museums today. Myron, like other Greek artists, was fascinated by the human form. He carefully sculpted every muscle of an athlete preparing to throw a discus. The Greeks greatly admired physical fitness, and some scholars think that *Discobolus* was meant to show more of the ideal athlete's build and muscle structure than the actual technique used by discus throwers in ancient Greece. Athletes in those times may not have started each throw by holding the discus behind them, as the figure in *Discobolus* does. Most historians think ancient Greek discus throwers instead used a simple version of the modern throwing technique, but without the beginning spin. Whether *Discobolus* shows an actual throwing style from ancient Greek times or was merely meant to show off an athlete's muscles, the statue is one of the most recognizable works of art left from that era and is a fascinating link between ancient Greece and the modern sporting world.

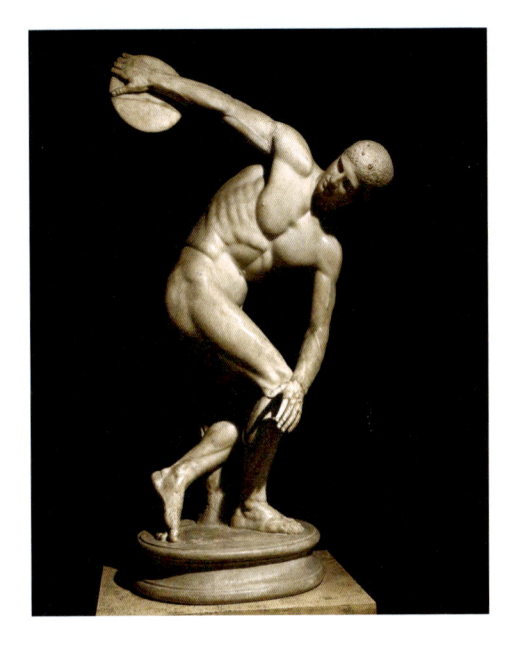

A replica of the famous Greek sculpture Discobolus *shows Myron's attention to the details of an athlete's physical form.*

The Olympics Are Born

The new sporting competition was called the Olympic Games, named after Mount Olympus, the highest mountain in Greece and the place the Greeks believed was the home of the gods. The Games were a chance for male Greek athletes to show off their running and throwing abilities in front of an audience. Every four years Greeks came from far and

A Greek vase depicts runners during an Olympic event. The Olympics in ancient Greece included jumping and throwing competitions as well as footraces.

wide to watch their fellow countrymen compete in footraces and throwing competitions. Olympic races included a long-distance, 3-mile run (4.8km) as well as a variety of shorter distances about equal to 880 yards (800m), 440 yards (400m), and the most popular event, the stade, a dash of about 220 yards (200m). The winner of the stade was called the fastest man of the games.

The shorter races at these early Olympics were run in lanes. About sixteen to twenty runners competed in a race, one runner per lane. If more than twenty racers signed up, the race would be divided into smaller divisions, or heats, with the winners of each heat moving on to compete in the final round. The starting line was informal—usually just a line scratched in the dirt—and the races were not timed. Whoever crossed the finish line first was the winner.

"We have no means of estimating the performances of these athletes, as the ancients had no accurate timing methods," says historian Nigel B. Crowther. "Even if they had, they seem to have been more interested in the concept of man against man (to produce a winner), rather than in man against the clock."[1] Even though the footraces were not timed and records were not kept from competition to competition, the early Olympics were nevertheless an obvious basis for modern track-and-field events of today, in which races of 200, 400, and 800 meters are still among the most popular events for competitive track runners.

ANCIENT ORIGINS

The word *athlete* comes from the Greek word *athlos*, meaning a contest or competition.

The Greeks took part in throwing and jumping events in those early Olympic Games, as well. They competed to see who could project a javelin, or spear, the farthest. Some competitors also flung a flat, pancake-shaped object known as a discus. Athletes competed in the long jump, too, an event in which competitors took a running start, then leaped outward as far as they could before their feet hit the ground. Like the Greeks' footraces, the long jump, the javelin, and the discus are among the events track-and-field competitors still compete in today.

The Olympic Games were a Greek tradition for about a thousand years. But in 330 A.D., the European world was changing in terms of politics and religion. The Greeks were no longer the war power they had once been, and many Europeans did not like the Greeks' pagan religion, which worshipped many different gods. The Olympic Games were seen as a pagan festival and were eventually forbidden. Formal track-and-field competitions became a phenomenon of ancient history. But people had seemingly developed a natural curiosity to see who was the fastest runner or the strongest thrower or the best jumper in civilized society. "Above all," says classical history professor David C. Young, "the Olympics were a showcase for human physical excellence. ... They passed beyond the athletic events proper to exemplify, even to symbolize, all of ancient Greek civilization at its best."[2] Eventually, this interest in amazing athletic feats would bring about a return of organized competitions for human strength and speed.

Track Comes Back

In the early 1800s, about fifteen hundred years after the end of the Greek Olympics, the United States was a new country. It had recently gained independence from England, and people from Europe and elsewhere in the world were immigrating to the new land by the thousands. American pioneers were exploring their new nation, building cities, and traveling. People felt free to be anything they wanted to be, and one of the new "jobs" that appealed to many was being a professional runner. Athletes roamed the country, competed in races, and earned money by winning bets. Races became such popular events at town picnics and other kinds of gatherings that business owners began sponsoring races and offering prizes. More and more runners showed up to compete for the winnings, and the good ones were able to earn a living with their feet. By the 1850s track-and-field sporting events were almost as popular in the United States

Crowds cheer on the competitors in a walking race in New York City in 1879. Track-and-field events were popular among sports fans in the United States as far back as the early 1800s.

as horse races were. Spectators paid for admission to watch the competitions. Organizers paid the athletes who competed. Being an athlete became a true profession. "Competitive running, throwing, and jumping events and organized track and field are among the older sporting events in the United States," says Joseph Turrini, an assistant professor of information science. "The most successful competitors were among the first professional athletes and sports stars in the country."[3]

During and after the Civil War, however, American track and field changed. Until then, it had been a sport with almost no formal rules or regulations. Distances that were run, jumped, or thrown were not standardized, and good records were seldom kept. "Athletes throughout the country claimed to be champions or record holders at particular distances," says Turrini, but "the self-proclaimed titles and record times held no legitimacy and often conflicted."[4] There was clearly a need for an organization to regulate and standardize track-and-field events. Therefore, in 1888 the Amateur Athletic Union of the United States (AAU) was formed. It not only set standard rules for track-and-field competitions, it forbade any track-and-field athlete to make money at the sport. In fact, it forbade any track athlete to make money doing anything, even working at another profession. The AAU believed that earning money would lead to cheating and would destroy the honesty and integrity of the athletes. But the amateur rule meant that anyone who had to work for a living was excluded from competing in track and field. For the most part, only those who did not have to work—namely, wealthy citizens and college students who were the sons of wealthy citizens—could participate in the sport. Under the AAU's new rules, women were excluded from competing altogether.

Return of the Olympics

For decades in the United States the amateur rule probably kept many would-be American track stars from competing in events. But just before the turn of the twentieth century, an important event occurred overseas. A French aristocrat named Pierre de Coubertin became dismayed by the lack of physical activity he was noticing among young French people. An avid historian, de Coubertin knew all about the Olympic Games of ancient Greece, and he decided to revive the Olympics in modern times to renew his countrymen's interest in athletic training and competition. He formed a committee with representatives from a dozen different countries, and in 1896 the first modern Olympic Games were held in Athens, Greece. "For de Coubertin, whose main aims were educational, the Olympic Games were to be seen as an advertisement of sport to youth, and the athletes participating in the Olympic Games seen as role models for a young generation,"[5] say sports philosophers Vassil Girginov and Jim Parry. The summer Olympics have been held every four years since that time except during World Wars I and II, and track-and-field events—many of

Discus thrower Robert Garrett of the United States won a gold medal at the first Olympic Games of the modern era, held in 1896 in Athens, Greece.

them dating back to ancient Greece—have kept their role as the heart of these worldwide athletic festivals. In keeping with de Coubertin's vision, Olympic track-and-field athletes have been role models for many generations of the world's youth.

Even after the rebirth of the Olympics made track and field a newly famous sport in the world, it was many decades until America's amateur rules—still in place even for Olympians—were finally abolished in 1978. At last, it was legal for American track-and-field athletes to earn money as professional competitors the way players of other sports like baseball and football had long been allowed to do. Women, too, were allowed to compete in an increas-

Marathon Madness

The modern running event with the most legendary ties to ancient Greek culture is the marathon, a 26-mile (42.19km) race measured not in seconds or minutes, but hours. The marathon was established during the 1896 revival of the Olympics to commemorate a Greek runner named Pheidippides, who ran a distance of about 25 miles (40.23km) from the Greek town of Marathon to the city of Athens to report an important battle victory. Upon arriving at his destination, the story goes, Pheidippides gasped a one-word message, "Nike" (meaning "victory"), before dying from exhaustion.

Today marathon competitions are held all over the world, such as the famous annual Boston Marathon in the United States and the London Marathon in England. The marathon is also an Olympic event. It is unique among running races in that about one in four men and one in five women in any given Olympics never reach the finish line, quitting from exhaustion, dehydration, or injury along the way. Those who do finish a marathon, however, succeed in a tremendous accomplishment. Their event goes miles beyond track and field. The marathon and the people who run it are in a class all their own.

ing number of Olympic track-and-field events throughout the twentieth century, opening up many new opportunities for female athletes. The revival of the Olympics ultimately brought about a major turn in worldwide sports, making track-and-field events a popular athletic endeavor in countries large and small. Today, runners, jumpers, and throwers compete at all levels, from junior high school all the way to the professional circuit.

Track and Field Today

In the past two millennia, from the time of the ancient Greeks to now, the world has witnessed incredible feats of human speed and power within the boundaries of track and field. The modern events differ in some ways from the races, jumps, and throwing competitions performed by the ancient Greeks and even the competitors at the first modern Olympics in 1896,

Sprinters dash to the finish within their designated lanes, a racing standard that dates back to the ancient Greeks.

but at the same time, most of the events of modern track and field are clear descendents of an earlier era. Running events are now held on an oval-shaped track, but this is divided into lanes much the way ancient Greek racers ran in lanes. When there are too many runners to fit on the track all at once, athletes compete in heats, and the winners of the heats race each other again to determine a winner. Field events such as jumping and throwing are still a part of track-and-field competitions, too, and the javelin and discus are two modern events that came directly from ancient Greece.

Changes have been made throughout the years to running surfaces, athletic techniques, and equipment. New events have been added. Modern technology also has earned a place at every track-and-field meet to time events and measure jumps and throws with great precision. National and world records are kept, too, chronicling the successes of amazing athletes in the modern era of track and field. Nevertheless, even in a rapidly changing world, track-and-field events are mostly the same athletic endeavors they have always been—tests of the physical limits and abilities of the human body. They are still competitions of sheer strength and speed. Modern athletes represent, as the Greeks did, the pinnacle of the human athletic form. And the modern world still marvels at the human physiology that makes up a superior track-and-field athlete.

CHAPTER **2**

The Race Is On: Sprints, Distance Races, and Hurdles

Today, much as in ancient Greece, there are two main divisions in every track-and-field tournament—races and field competitions. Many field events take place inside the boundaries of the oval-shaped track, but the track surface itself is devoted to showdowns between athletes who race to beat their competitors and set new records in their best events. These athletes combine the complex science of human physiology with the track surface's physical properties to achieve the greatest possible speed and endurance. Track races reveal all the abilities and limitations of the human body as it performs one of its most basic athletic movements—running.

Fast and Furious

There are two kinds of races in track—distance races, which require the ability to run multiple laps, and sprints, which test a runner's speed over a short distance. Sprints are races of up to one full lap around a standard track,

TRACK AND FIELD ARENA

The typical arena for track and field is divided into specific areas for each event, allowing the athletes plenty of safe competition space. Track lines are used to mark the starting points and race distances for specific running events.

- Pole Vault
- Discus and Hammer Throw
- Shot Put
- High Jump
- Javelin
- Long and Triple Jump

Length for the 100m race

Length for the 200m race

Length for the 400m race

Sprints are races of up to one full lap around a standard track, which is 400m (about 440yd) in length, or one-quarter of a mile. Half of a lap, or one length and one curve of the track, is 200m (about 220yd), and a quarter of a lap, or one straight section of the track, is 100m (about 110yd).

which is 400 meters, or about 440 yards, in length, or one quarter of a mile. Half of a lap, or one length and one curve of the track, is 200 meters, or 220 yards, and a quarter of a lap—one straight section of the track—is 100 meters, or about 110 yards. Sprinters can specialize in any of these three distances. The shortest race, 100 meters, determines the fastest runner of a track tournament or meet, because in this quick dash runners reach the highest speeds of any running event. The world's best 100-meter sprinters strive to set new records for the fastest speed ever accomplished by the human body, and the record holders are known as the world's fastest woman and man. When Jamaican sprinter Usain Bolt set a new world record in 2009 by running the 100-meter dash in 9.58 seconds, he ran faster than 23 miles per hour (37kph), a feat some experts had thought was impossible. "I never thought that I would see this even if I lived to be 100,"[6] said 81-year-old former U.S. Olympic men's track coach Mel Rosen after watching Bolt's record-shattering run.

On the Fast Track

All tracks are not created equal. They all have the same dimensions and shape, and most modern track surfaces are made of a flexible, durable polyurethane material that improves traction and is weatherproof. Yet runners tend to perform better on some tracks than others. One difference has to do with altitude, or how high a track sits above sea level. As altitude increases, the composition of the air changes, too. Air is made of molecules of gases, including oxygen, which tend to sink and become denser at a low altitude such as the bottom of a valley. At higher altitudes air is less dense, meaning there are fewer gas molecules in a given volume of air. Since muscles need oxygen to keep from feeling fatigued, runners in medium- and long-distance races feel tired sooner at higher altitudes where oxygen is less plentiful. Sprinters, however, who are slowed down by air resistance, find that less-dense air makes up for the lower oxygen level during short, fast races. Sprinters tend to run faster at high altitude with less air resistance, while long-distance runners tend to have their best races at lower altitudes where oxygen is in greater supply.

Anatomy of a Sprinter

Complicated scientific processes happen in a sprinter's body to achieve such tremendous running speed. In general, a runner relies on strong, well-developed skeletal muscles, the body's powerhouses, to propel him forward. Skeletal muscle is one of three types of muscle in the human body. The other two types, smooth muscle and cardiac muscle, exist in internal organs to move things such as food that is being digested or, in the case of cardiac muscle, to pump blood out of the heart. Smooth and cardiac muscles move involuntarily—a person does not have to think about them. Skeletal muscles, on the other hand, are voluntary, moving bones when the brain tells them to so the body can do things like run. They are also the body's biggest and most powerful muscles. They consist of groups of stretchy fibers, working somewhat like clumps of rubber bands. As these fibers stretch and contract, they pull into motion the bones of the body, such as the thighbones and shinbones of the leg. The fibers of skeletal muscles grow larger and stronger the more they are used, and the larger the muscle, the more power it can create. Sprinters develop

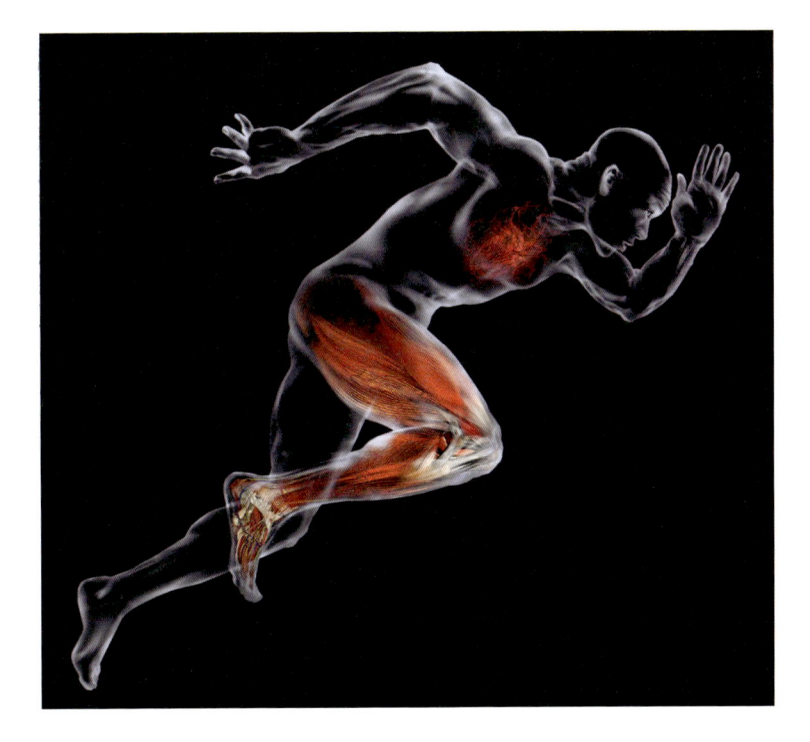

An illustration of a sprinter's form highlights the skeletal muscles of the leg and the cardiac muscle, both of which are critical to giving a runner speed, power, and endurance.

SPLIT-SECOND STARTS

.17

Number of seconds after the starting pistol fires to begin a sprint race for the sprinter's hands to leave the ground, .29 seconds for the rear foot to leave the blocks, and .44 seconds for the front foot to push off.

massive muscles, especially in their hips and thighs, to help them move fast. "The leg strength of sprinters is greater than that of distance runners and of the general population," says sports scientist Clyde Williams. "The large muscle mass that is characteristic of elite sprinters contributes to their running success because it allows them to generate large forces quickly."[7]

The large muscles in a sprinter's body need a large source of energy to make the body move. Muscles get their energy from adenosine triphosphate (ATP) molecules, which work like tiny batteries within the body's cells. When cells need energy to do something, they break apart ATP molecules to release the stored energy. Many cells breaking apart ATP molecules all at once—such as the cells of a contracting muscle—will release enough energy to allow the body to perform a large movement such as running. Eventually, when all of a cell's ATP molecules are broken down, it has no more energy to give. It must replenish its stores of ATP by digesting sugar from food and using the sugar's energy to put ATP molecules back together. These "recharged" ATP molecules then store energy again, but the process requires more time than the mere seconds it takes for a sprinter to finish a race.

When muscle cells break down ATP faster than they can make more of it, the muscles run out of energy. The result is fatigue, or the feeling of being too tired to continue moving. Because sprinters accelerate as fast as possible, their muscles use up ATP very quickly. Sprinters cannot run at top speed for very long. "Sprint running is characterized by a constantly changing speed with an initial rapid acceleration followed by a subsequent decline in running velocity as the onset of fatigue develops," says sports and recreation scientist Henry Lakomy. "Maximum speed cannot be maintained during even the shortest sprint; power output in humans decreases rapidly with increasing duration of effort."[8] Nevertheless, the explosive power in a sprinter's muscles is enough to reach incredible speed over a short distance and propel him to the finish line.

A Sprint, from Start to Finish

The muscles of a sprinter's body are poised to begin working even before the race starts. A sudden sound, traditionally a blast from a starting pistol, begins races in track and field. In the seconds before the starting pistol is fired, racers crouch behind the starting line, the balls of their feet pressed against two metal surfaces called starting blocks. One leg is farther back than the other, simulating a step being taken while running. The racers' fingers are on the ground, pressed against the starting line. Their hips are raised into the air. Their shoulders lean forward. Every muscle is tense, waiting to react to the sound of the signal and surge into motion.

Once the shot is fired, a sprinter launches out of starting position. Both feet shove off the starting blocks. The leg that is farther back is the first to swing forward at the hip,

A sprinter takes her initial stride off of the starting block, with her torso leaning forward as she uses her energy to build speed.

beginning the first step of the race. The initial strides of a sprint are run with the torso, or the part of the body above the waist, leaning forward and almost parallel to the ground. It takes energy to shift the weight of the torso from a crouch to a full standing position, and the sprinter instead uses all his energy during the first few steps of the race to reach top leg speed. About the first 20 meters, or 66 feet, of a 100-meter sprinting race is spent accelerating. As the runner approaches top speed, he raises his torso up to a more natural angle for running, and at this point, the race moves into its second phase. "The sprint is made up of several sections, and is not, as the casual observer might conclude, a simple race between gun and tape," says Williams. "The elite sprinter must be able to achieve maximal efficiency over each section of the race if he or she seeks to cross the finish line ahead of the competition."[9] Once the runner has fully accelerated, he faces the difficult task of maintaining that pace. Several factors start to work against the athlete, making it difficult to keep going at top speed for very long.

Speed Sappers

Air resistance is one element that slows the sprinter down. Air is a gas, and like any other form of matter such as a solid or a liquid, gases have mass—a certain number of tiny molecules per unit of area. As a person runs, the molecules in the air have to be pushed aside to let the runner through. The pressure of air molecules against the forward motion of a body is called air resistance. The faster the body moves, the more air resistance is created against it. By halfway through a 100-meter sprint, a racer running at top speed is moving fast and therefore experiencing more air resistance than at the start of the race when he was just beginning to gain speed. This increase in air resistance is one force that works to slow him down.

Another factor sprinters struggle against is friction, or the force of one object moving in a sliding motion against another as their surfaces come into contact. With every step of a race, a runner's feet create friction as they strike against the ground. Good sprinters try to lessen the impact of each footfall by pulling back on the foot just before it hits the track. This softens the blow of the foot against the ground, so the runner loses less momentum (a measurement of forward motion based on a moving object's mass and speed) to the force of friction than if each foot hit the ground with a hard, jarring motion that slowed forward progress. Nevertheless, a runner's every step creates *some* friction, and this, combined with air resistance, works to slow a sprinter down in the second half of a race.

The third and most important factor that affects a sprinter's speed, of course, is the loss of muscle energy. The runner who reaches top speed the fastest and has the strength and ATP stores to maintain that speed throughout the race will usually be the first to cross the finish line. "One of the distinguishing features of the world's best sprinters is that they are not only able to run fast, but also to maintain these speeds throughout the latter part of a race,"[10] says Williams. The difference between winning first or second place in a sprint may be a mere hundredth of a second, so the combination of running form, technique, and power must be perfectly balanced. The tiniest flaw in any of these factors could result in losing the race.

A sprinter breaks through the finish-line tape just ahead of his opponents. A runner's speed is affected by air resistance, friction, and the loss of muscle energy through the course of a race.

The Race Is On: Sprints, Distance Races, and Hurdles 27

Going the Distance

Not all track-and-field races are sprints. Middle-distance and long-distance races require different running techniques, and even different kinds of muscle. Distance races include the 800-meter race of two laps, or half a mile. Other races include the 1 mile (1600m, or four laps) and the 2 mile (3200m, or eight laps). Runners of longer distances rely less on speed and more on endurance, or the ability of the body

Distance runner Hicham El Guerrouj, whose lean build is typical of those in his sport, holds the world record for the fastest mile.

to keep expending physical effort for a long time. Unlike sprinters, who use up all of their muscles' energy stores rapidly during short runs at top speed, runners of longer distances use up energy stores less quickly because they move at a slower pace over a longer period of time. Endurance allows distance runners to conserve energy so they can keep running for several laps around the track instead of becoming fatigued after a fast short distance.

> # HALF-AND-HALF
> **50 percent**
> Approximate percentage of a runner's stride that involves contact with the ground. The other 50 percent is air time between strides.

People who are good sprinters rarely make good distance runners, and few distance runners are also good at reaching the explosive speeds of sprinters. Muscles of distance runners work somewhat differently than the muscles of sprinters. The stretchy fibers that make up skeletal muscles come in two types. Type I fibers are called slow-twitch fibers. Type II fibers are called fast-twitch fibers. The term *twitch* refers to how fast the muscle fibers can contract, or shorten, to pull the bones they are attached to into motion. Fast-twitch, type II fibers tend to be bulky and powerful and can release a lot of ATP very quickly for fast muscle movement. These powerful fibers are most common in sprinters, but they have disadvantages—once developed through weight training, they are bulky and heavier to carry around, and they also fatigue very quickly. "Only in events from the 800 meters on down can runners offset the gravitational pull of additional body mass with the improvements in power that come from strength training,"[11] says distance-running coach and exercise physiologist Roy Benson. Slow-twitch, type I muscle fibers, on the other hand, take a bit longer to contract and move the body's bones, but they do not use up ATP nearly as quickly as fast-twitch fibers do. Distance runners, whose lean muscles tend to have more of the slender, slow-twitch fibers, take off with less power but are able to sustain a certain speed for a distance of two, four, eight, or more laps around the track before their muscles tire out.

Distance runners do not have the same explosive speed as sprinters, but that does not mean they are slow. Many

Olympic-level competitors can run 1 mile (1.6km) in under 4 minutes. Hicham El Guerrouj of Morocco set the world mile record at 3 minutes, 43 seconds in 1999, keeping an average pace of more than 15 miles per hour (24kph) for four entire laps—the fastest recorded mile ever run by a human being.

Running for Agility

Some track races are competitions of sheer human speed, others of endurance. A third type of running competition requires both speed and endurance, as well as the agility to leap over obstacles at a dead run. Athletes who run this unique type of race are called hurdlers, and their races have the most technical demands of any event that takes place on the track.

Hurdlers rely on both speed and timing to perfect their racing technique.

Hurdle races are basically sprints but with an extra challenge built in—racers must jump over ten separate hurdles before reaching the finish line. Hurdles are approximately waist-high obstacles spaced evenly over the race distance—about every 10 meters, or 33 feet, in a 100-meter hurdle race,

30 Track and Field

for example, and every 40 meters, or 131 feet, in a 400-meter hurdle race. The hurdle is made from an L-shaped frame with a plastic crosspiece along the top. Racers must stay in their own lane, leap over each hurdle, avoid tripping and falling, and complete the race as fast as possible.

Technique is extremely important in a hurdle race. "Hurdling is one of the most complex events in track and field," says sports reporter and author Ed Housewright. "Athletes must carefully measure and rehearse their steps between hurdles to achieve maximum rhythm and speed. … To clear a hurdle properly, they must jump the right height at the right time. If they jump too high, they'll expend too much effort and lose time. If they jump too low, they'll hit the hurdle."[12] The best hurdlers time their jumps perfectly, lifting their front leg off the ground just enough to clear the hurdle and then lifting their back knee, ankle, and foot over the top. An experienced hurdler lands smoothly, stepping right into the next stride. Expert hurdlers are so good at jumping in mid-stride that their heads and shoulders barely rise as they clear each hurdle. The whole process requires a great deal of practice. "Nobody becomes a first-rate hurdler overnight,"[13] says Housewright.

The combination of sprinting and leaping in a hurdle race requires speed, endurance, and coordination. Hurdle races also demonstrate the importance of standardized measurements in track events. The dimensions and layout of a racing track and everything on it must be precise and exact for runners to practice and compete fairly. Consistent measurement is one of the most important aspects of this sport.

Dimensions of Running Track

A standard track is oval in shape, marked usually into eight running lanes, each 48 inches (1.2m) wide. For sprint races a runner must stay in his or her lane through the entire race, and for fairness the race must be exactly the same distance for each runner. In the 100-meter dash, the starting line is at one end of a straight length of the track, and the finish line is at the other end. This is the easiest race to measure. Sprints that include one or more curves of the track, such as the

200-meter sprint (covering half the track, or one curve and one straight) and the 400-meter sprint (one full lap, or two curves and two straights), are trickier. All runners cannot start on the same straight line in these races, because every lane of the track actually covers a different distance.

A track is really a set of concentric ovals—each oval shares the same center point, but the farther it is from the center, the longer it is. "The running track is only 400m around in lane 1," says youth track coach Gary Barber. In each subsequent lane the distance around the track is about 7 meters longer, because the oval is slightly bigger. Therefore, at the start of a 400-meter race, which involves two turns of the track, "each runner will be placed 7m in front of the runner behind them," Barber says. "This 'staggered start' as it is known ensures that each [athlete] runs the 400m."[14] The seeming head start of

Coming Around the Bend

The shape of the track can create special challenges for runners, who must adapt their running technique to navigate the curves. A moving object's natural tendency is to continue forward in a straight line, so running on a curve requires extra energy. The athlete must lean into the curve to compensate for the force that is trying to pull his center of gravity back onto a straight course. He pumps his outside arm (the one closest to the outer edge of the track) across his body to help him balance during the lean. When he reaches the end of the curve and heads back into a straight portion of the track, he receives an extra surge of energy as his body stops fighting the curve and returns to the straight line of motion it favors. Good runners accelerate as they come out of a curve, channeling this burst of energy into greater speed. The shorter the race, the greater the runners' speed on the curves, and the stronger the natural pull they will feel to go straight. Expertly navigating the track's curves can shave precious fractions of seconds off the race time and is a hallmark of an experienced runner.

the runners in outer lanes actually compensates for the larger circumference of, or total distance around, each consecutive lane. By the time they reach the finish line (which is always at the end of a straight portion of the track), the runners have all covered exactly the same distance.

At the Finish Line

Each race can have only one winner. Just as it is essential to make sure that track distances are measured precisely, timing is extremely important as well. Not only does accurate timing help determine the winner if a race has a close finish, it also indicates whether a record has been broken. A string used to be stretched across the finish line to

A photo finish indicates the winner of a race by a narrow margin that may be undetectable to the naked eye. Race officials rely upon sophisticated finish-line cameras that can measure time to one one-thousandth of a second.

The Race Is On: Sprints, Distance Races, and Hurdles

determine who finished the race first, but in modern times there is a far more accurate system involving a camera and a digital timer. The camera lens is aimed at the finish line, and a timer integrated into the camera records the exact moment each runner finishes the race. Since races are often won and records broken by very small margins, it is critical to have a standard procedure for measuring time and to be able to check the results. Modern finish-line cameras can measure time to one one-thousandth of a second, or 0.001. Each finish is recorded so that close races can be played back in slow motion and race officials can determine who actually crossed the finish line first. The starting pistol (or other starting sound) automatically triggers the digital race timers to start, ensuring that each runner is timed from exactly the same instant. Today's digital systems for timing races are more sensitive and accurate than any race measurement method in history. People have become capable of timing and measuring human performance in such detail that world records are often broken by only a tiny fraction of a second. Technology and precise measurement have become as vital to track events as the legs that propel runners toward the finish line.

CHAPTER 3

Up, Up, and Away: Jumping Events and the Pole Vault

Precisely measured races around the track test the physical limits of human speed and endurance, but they are not the only type of event in which track-and-field athletes compete for superior measurements. The "field" portion of the sport involves other types of events, many of which also date back to the first Olympic tournaments of the ancient Greeks. Several field events, many of which take place on the inner portion of the track, are tests not of how fast a person can run but how well an athlete can defy the force of gravity in order to accomplish the highest or farthest jumps. Track-and-field jumpers can compete in the long jump, the triple jump, the high jump or the pole vault, all events that require considerable strength and skill to stay in the air longer than any other competitor.

The Pull of the Earth

The main external force working against jumpers is gravity, a natural attraction between everything in the universe that consists of matter and therefore has mass. The larger the object, the stronger its gravitational pull on smaller objects

A long jumper's power and speed send her body into flight, but her landing is the result of the earth's gravitational pull.

nearby. Everything on the surface of Earth is far smaller than the planet itself, so these objects are constantly pulled toward Earth's surface through the force of gravity. If a ball is thrown straight up in the air, it will reach a certain height as it briefly conquers Earth's gravitational force, but soon, gravity will pull the ball back down to the ground again. If the same ball is thrown forward, it will travel in a fairly straight line for some distance, but eventually gravity will make the ball arc back down to the ground. Similarly, human beings can reach only a certain vertical height or horizontal distance in the air before gravity pulls them down again. In the sport of track-and-field, jumpers compete to see who can use strength and skill to conquer the pull of gravity for the longest possible time. "Top jumpers almost appear to be flying, suspended off the earth's surface as they strive for another fraction of an inch," says Ed Housewright. "Athletes must temporarily overcome gravity to jump high or long."[15]

Just as every object that has mass is affected by gravity, every object also has what is called a center of gravity. This is the single point within the object at which its total mass and weight are evenly distributed. If the object were placed on top of a stick or a pole, the center of gravity is the exact point at which the object would balance perfectly without toppling over. In the human body, which is symmetrical (the same shape on the left side and the right side, if the body were folded exactly in half from left to right), the center of gravity is located at about the height of the waist and on the midpoint of the body between the left side and the right—approximately at the navel. In order for a person to change position, such as in running or jumping, she has to move her center of gravity in the direction she wants to go. Track-and-field jumpers must develop the right techniques

The Buckeye Bullet

When the 1936 summer Olympics took place in Berlin, Germany, German leader Adolf Hitler anticipated sweeping wins by "Aryan" Germans, those who had light skin, light hair, and light eyes. The United States brought forth an African American sprinter who turned that notion on its head. His name was Jesse Owens, and he came from Ohio State University with a big reputation to defend. Nicknamed Ohio State's "Buckeye Bullet," Owens once set three world records and tied a fourth in the space of forty-five minutes during a single track-and-field meet. Owens won the 100-meter dash, the 200-meter dash, the 400-meter relay, and the long jump at the Games, becoming the first athlete to win four gold medals in a single Olympics (a record that stood until American sprinter Carl Lewis tied Owens's Olympic medal count in 1984). The world was in awe of Owens, who today is still regarded as one of the greatest Olympians of all time. After retiring from competition, Owens spent his life working with underprivileged youth. In 1976 he was awarded the Medal of Freedom, the highest honor the United States can bestow on a civilian. Owens died in 1980 but left a heroic legacy both on and off the track.

African American sprinter Jesse Owens won four gold medals at the 1936 Olympic Games in Berlin, Germany.

to shift their body's center of gravity in the correct outward and upward directions so that their body can stay off the ground for the longest possible time. The most successful jumpers are usually the athletes with the most control over their center of gravity.

Jumping for Distance

There are two main types of jumps in track and field, challenging athletes to shift their center of gravity in different directions. Jumpers can propel themselves either vertically, straight up in the air, or horizontally, in a direction parallel to the ground. The long jump and the triple jump test a person's ability to jump a horizontal distance after a running start. In both events athletes have a short length of track, 40 meters, that they use to accelerate before making their leap. In the long

A composite photo shows an athlete in the various stages of a long jump, from the beginning of his leap to the landing.

jump, an athlete sprints to build as much speed as possible before launching out over the sandpit where he will land. In the triple jump, an athlete sprints, then begins a series of three separate launches. First he skips forward off of one foot, landing on the same foot. Then he takes one long stride, landing on the opposite foot. From that foot, he launches into the third and final leap, landing in the sandpit.

In both styles of jumping, the approach determines how far the jumper will travel before gravity pulls him back down. For long jumpers, the length of the jump is directly related to the speed the athlete is able to build up during the approach. The athlete generates velocity during the sprint, which in turn creates momentum. Velocity is the speed at which an object (in this case, the runner) is changing position in a forward direction. The greater the runner's velocity at the instant he begins his leap, the greater his body's momentum will be, and the farther he will travel horizontally until gravity pulls him back down to earth. "In a mechanical sense, success simply means having a large horizontal velocity and plenty of time in the air, because velocity (meters per second) multiplied by time (seconds) gives us distance (meters)," says kinesiologist Arthur Chapman, who specializes in the study of human movement. Because greater speed at takeoff means more distance in the air, "it is no surprise that good long jumpers are good to excellent sprinters, without exception,"[16] Chapman says.

A triple jumper, in contrast, combines velocity and momentum with extra motions of the arms, legs, and torso before jumping. The triple jumper drives his body upward during the hopping and skipping phase of the approach. By swinging the limbs just before the moment of takeoff, the jumper is able to move his center of gravity higher. This combination of height and velocity during the third and final jump contributes to the amount of time it takes for gravity to pull the athlete back down to the ground. "The triple jump

BAR STARS

The term *raising the bar*, which means raising expectations for a person's performance, comes from the high jump event in track and field, because after each successful round of jumping, the crossbar is raised a bit higher.

is uniquely different from the other jumping events in track and field," says college track coach Mark Guthrie. "It can be best compared to a floor routine in gymnastics. ... To be proficient in the triple jump, an athlete not only needs to possess speed and explosiveness, but body awareness and balance to perform a rhythmical and controlled effort."[17]

A horizontal jump like the long jump or triple jump takes the shape of a low arc. It begins where the jumper leaves the ground, curves upward slightly as the jumper's body gains height during the leap, and then curves back down to the earth. The long jumper relies mostly on momentum to carry her forward faster but in a lower arc before she hits the ground. The triple jumper relies more on gaining height in the jump, thus creating a higher arc to travel a farther distance. Whether the jumper focuses more on velocity and forward momentum or more on driving the body's center of gravity upward as high as possible, the amount of time spent in the air will always be limited by the incvitable pull of gravity. Both styles of horizontal jumping are difficult, and they showcase how physically fit a person must be to defy the earth's strong pull on the things around it.

Jumping for Height

The long jump and the triple jump measure how far a person can leap from a given starting point. Another kind of jump measures how high a person can soar—specifically, how high the athlete can raise his center of gravity off the ground. This event is the high jump, and athletes who perform it rely less on speed than on technique to move their entire body to a height level with or even above their own head.

In the high jump, leaps are not measured by how far the athlete can lift his feet off the ground but by whether his entire body can clear a horizontal pole propped up on two vertical stands. During a track-and-field competition, the high jump crossbar starts at a low position, usually one that most jumpers can leap over successfully. After each jumper has a turn, the pole is raised a couple of centimeters higher. Competitors who cannot clear the pole after each time it is raised are eliminated, until one competitor remains—the athlete who jumped the highest. Some high jumpers can clear seemingly impossible heights. In 1993 Javier Sotomayor of Cuba completed a record-setting high jump of 2.45 meters, or 8 feet and one-half inch, becoming the first high jumper in history to break the 8-foot barrier. Sotomayor is 6 feet 4 inches tall, so he jumped a vertical distance about 30 percent greater than his own height. Defying gravity to move the entire body to a height far above one's own head requires great strength and skill, and high jumpers like Sotomayor accomplish this amazing feat by expertly controlling their body's center of gravity.

High jumpers can use any technique they want during the jump as long as every part of their body clears the horizontal crossbar without knocking it down. The most popu-

Cuban Javier Sotomayor was the first high jumper to clear a jump of more than 8 feet in competition. A high jumper's success is affected not only by muscle strength, but also by his ability to master his body's center of gravity.

Up, Up, and Away: Jumping Events and the Pole Vault

lar technique begins with an approach of several bounding steps toward the bar in a J-shaped run that starts straight and curves at the end. The straight portion of the running approach helps to build speed and momentum, and the curve naturally pulls the jumper's body into a slight turn so that one shoulder is facing the crossbar. The jumper then uses the muscles of the legs and buttocks to spring into the air. His head, shoulders, and torso clear the crossbar backward with his chest and belly toward the sky, draping at the waist to pull his hips up and over the bar. Once his midsection has cleared the crossbar, the jumper bends at the waist, drawing his knees toward his chest to snap the legs and feet up and

Not a Flop

Before 1968 high jumpers took a head-on approach to the crossbar. A jumper ran toward it and leapt upward and sideways, sailing over the bar facedown. It seemed the most natural and effective way to jump. Then a college track athlete named Dick Fosbury developed a completely different technique—he twisted his body in the last step of his running approach and turned around to leap over the bar faceup and backward. Fosbury's odd-looking method might have been funny to his rivals if it had not been so successful. He won the high jump that year at the national collegiate track-and-field finals and went on to win a gold medal in the high jump at the 1968 Olympics.

In college, while studying physics and engineering, Fosbury had calculated that his new technique made him far less likely to hit the crossbar, since each segment of his body—shoulders, hips, and legs—could be lifted over the bar separately in an arching motion instead of all at once in a straight line. Ultimately, the new style allowed him to clear the bar more than 1 foot (30cm) higher than when he used the old method. After Fosbury beat out his 1968 Olympic competitors, other high jumpers started trying his technique. The Fosbury flop is now the standard technique most high jumpers use.

THE FOSBURY FLOP

To be successful in the pole vault event, jumpers must shift their center of gravity upward in order to defy gravity and clear the horizontal bar. The most common technique used today is the Fosbury Flop.

over the pole. The jumper lands on his shoulders and usually moves into a backward somersault once the jump is complete (he lands on thick, soft mats so that he does not get hurt). If the jump is a success, no part of the athlete's body will nudge the crossbar and knock it down. He then proceeds to the next round of jumping, in which the bar is moved a little higher.

A successful high jump requires perfect control of the body's center of gravity, which has to move over the pole. The earth's gravitational pull tugs vertically downward on objects at their center of gravity. Since in humans this is about the point of the navel, a high jumper must force his belly button high enough in the air to clear the horizontal bar. It is almost as if the jumper imagines having a string connected to his navel, pulling him upward in the middle. Even if the jumper's belly clears the bar as he arches his back up and over it, he might still nudge the bar with his legs or feet and spoil the jump. However, if a jumper's navel, or center of gravity, does not get high enough to clear the bar in the first place, he cannot possibly complete the jump. The high

Up, Up, and Away: Jumping Events and the Pole Vault 43

jump, then, requires not only the muscle strength to launch the body high into the air against the force of gravity, but also an instinctive understanding and control of balance and one's center of gravity. High jumpers display great finesse and gracefulness. "Track and field is a beautiful sport, and the high jump is one of the most exciting and remarkable of the events in track and field," says college jumping coach Cliff Rovelto. "An athlete flying over a bar that is quite frequently well overhead is as impressive a feat to watch as any in sport."[18]

Vetting the Pole Vault

The high jump requires a particular type of strength and skill, almost gymnastic in nature. The pole vault, the other type of field event that tests vertical jumping ability, involves many of the same skills as high jumping—particularly the ability to control and maneuver the body around its center of gravity. Like the high jump, the pole vault requires jumpers to shift their center of gravity upward in order to clear a horizontal bar without knocking it down. Like long jumpers, pole-vaulters sprint during the approach of their jump to build speed that will help propel them into a leap. Unlike any other jumping event, however, the pole vault requires athletes to reach an altitude that may be several times their own height. The world record in the pole vault is more than 20 feet (6.1m) in the air.

Jumpers achieve such elevation by combining their own strength and speed with a special tool—a flexible pole ranging in length from about 10 to 16 feet (3m–5m) and made of fiberglass and carbon fiber. When jammed into the ground ahead of the jumper, the pole flexes to spring the athlete high into the air, where he strives to clear a crossbar without knocking it down. "Pole vault demands gymnastic ability and a certain degree of fearlessness,"[19] says Gerry Carr, a track-and-field coach and former Olympic discus thrower.

A successful pole vault uses two types of energy—potential and kinetic. Energy is the ability to do physical work, such as moving an object from place to place, and it comes in many different forms. One form, potential energy, is energy stored in an object. A stretched rubber band has potential energy, for example, because if released, the rubber band will instantly shrink back to a non-stretched state. A roller-coaster car perched at the top of a steep hill also has potential energy, as does a spring that is being held closed. Kinetic energy, meanwhile, is the energy of any object that is in motion. When the roller coaster car plummets down the hill or when the tension on the spring is released, the object then has kinetic energy, or energy of motion.

> # GOLDEN GIRL
>
> Women were not allowed to compete in the pole vault until the Olympics in Sydney, Australia, in 2000. The first gold medal winner in the women's event was American Stacy Dragila.

Pole-vaulters use the pole to create both potential and kinetic energy. At the start of a jump, a pole-vaulter stands at the far end of the approach runway, gripping one end of the pole with hands spread wide apart. The pole is lifted off the ground and extends out in front of the jumper as he begins his approach. The jumper builds as much speed as possible by sprinting down the runway, which, as in the long jump, is approximately 40 meters long. When he reaches the end of the runway he plants the front end of his pole into a wedge-shaped depression in the runway called the pole box, which instantly stops the forward motion of the pole. Since the runner is still moving forward, the pole bends, flexing backward. This goes against its natural tendency to be straight, so the bent pole is loaded with potential energy. "The flexible pole can be thought of as an energy storage mechanism," says Chapman. "The force of the vaulter on the pole is increasing potential (strain) in the pole."[20]

Once the pole is lodged in the pole box and bent into a curve, the vaulter lifts one knee and pushes hard off the ground with the other foot, still gripping the top of the pole in both hands. As the flexed pole straightens, its potential energy changes to kinetic energy, and the vaulter uses this energy of motion to gain more height in the jump. He drives his hips (and center of gravity) upward and points his feet toward the sky as he rises, so that at the top of the jump—when the pole is completely straight—the jumper's body is vertical and upside down. In this position, his center of

The potential energy in the vaulter's bent pole turns to kinetic energy as the pole straightens, helping to launch the athlete over the crossbar.

gravity—located near his waist—is ideally higher than the horizontal crossbar he must jump over. He swings his body up and over the crossbar, beginning his descent feetfirst. He simultaneously pushes the pole out and away from him so that it does not fall forward and knock down the crossbar used to measure the jump. The vaulter falls feetfirst, to land on a mat below, having completed one of the most technically difficult and dangerous maneuvers in track and field. "Pole vaulting launches athletes to great heights and can be one of the most exciting jumping events," says Housewright, but he adds that pole-vaulting is not for the faint of heart. "Naturally, leaping that high might scare some people, for good reason ... competitors are occasionally seriously injured or even killed when they fail to land on the mat."[21]

Lords of Leaping

Jumps are unique among the many events of track and field because they require a special blend of strength, coordination, and instinctive understanding of the location and position of one's body and center of gravity. Endless hours of practice teach jumpers exactly how many steps to take during the approach and precisely how to make the body move during the jump itself. Jumpers re-create these practiced movements over and over, striving for a jump that is just a little higher or a little farther than their previous best attempt. This well-practiced precision can make jumping events look almost effortless to spectators, but they require many different scientific processes dealing with energy, gravity, and human structure and biology. Jumping is among the most technical and challenging of all track-and-field events.

CHAPTER 4

A Toss-Up: Shot Put, Hammer Throw, Discus, and Javelin

Many competitions in track and field test athletes' ability to compete within the limits of certain physical boundaries, such as the curve of the track or the parameters of the jumping pit. Other events require athletes to aim *past* boundaries. These athletes are throwers, and their events—another part of the "field" portion of track and field—require them to fling, spin, or shove an object through the air as they compete for the longest throwing distance. The task requires a great deal of strength, and throwers often have bulky, muscular bodies. In throwing events, however, basic principles of physics are also very important. The best throwers are not merely the strongest, but the ones who understand concepts like gravity, aerodynamics, momentum, and centripetal force. They learn to command or overcome such forces as they compete in one of four throwing events: the shot put, the hammer throw, the discus, or the javelin.

Throwing Stones

Like many events in track and field, throwing has a long history in human athletics, and the origins of the shot put date back thousands of years. The event likely evolved from ancient rock-throwing contests between chieftains of tribes in the British Isles as they competed to see which leader was most powerful. In the Middle Ages similar contests were held to see who could hurl a cannon ball the farthest using a pushing motion called a "put" (thus, the term "shot put"). When the modern Olympics were revived in 1896, the shot put was included as one of the events, and it has remained a popular contest of brute strength ever since. "If athletics measures the limits of various forms of human performance, what could be more basic than the simple competition of who can toss a heavy object, or stone, the farthest?" say professional shot-putter Ramona Pagel and her husband and coach, Kent Pagel. "The sheer force and physical explosiveness necessary to propel a heavy object within a short space

A shot putter tucks her throwing hand next to her chin as she spins to build momentum and maximize projection speed during the throw.

A Toss-Up: Shot Put, Hammer Throw, Discus, and Javelin

FANTASTIC FOUR

2

Number of track-and-field athletes to have ever won Olympic gold medals in the same event in four consecutive Olympic tournaments: American long jumper Carl Lewis and American discus thrower Al Oerter.

has produced a fascination that has lasted and increased into the modern Olympic era."[22]

The shot put involves holding a heavy ball, usually made of lead, to the side of one's chin and then pushing it away from the body for distance. In professional track-and-field competitions, the men's shot put weighs 16 pounds (7.3kg) and the women's weighs 8 pounds (3.6kg). The heavy metal ball has no aerodynamic properties, meaning that its round shape does not interact with the force of the air around it to help it stay aloft. Rather, the shot put responds to two primary forces—the energy the thrower transfers to it before sending it into the air, and gravity, the inevitable pull of the shot back down to the ground once it is thrown. Athletes concentrate on building momentum before the throw, and then shoving the shot put into the air at an ideal angle so that it travels as far as possible before gravity puts an end to its airborne path.

An object that has mass requires force, or energy, to be applied in order for it to move, a principle first described by physicist Sir Isaac Newton in the late 1600s. Newton was the scientist who pointed out that everything with mass also has inertia, or a natural resistance to force. In other words, a resting object will not move unless energy is used to put it in motion. The more mass a resting object has, the heavier it is, and the more energy it will take to move it. Since a shot put is heavy, a lot of energy is needed to send it upward and outward away from the ground. Shot-putters cannot get a running start to build momentum for the throw, however. They are given only a small circle, 7 feet (2.1m) in diameter, from which to throw, and if they step outside it, they are disqualified. Shot-putters have learned to use the space inside this circle to help their body gain momentum, thus generating more energy to pass on to the shot, overcoming its inertia at the instant it is tossed.

One way to gain momentum within the 7-foot circle is to start at the back of the circle, opposite where the throw will take place, and shuffle rapidly to the front before making the put. This gives the athlete a bit more forward momentum compared to standing still at the front of the circle before flinging the shot. Even better than the back-to-front shuffle, a spinning approach allows the athlete to gain even more speed and momentum right before the throw. Energy from the thrower's spinning body is then transferred to the shot put, increasing its speed once it is thrown. This projection speed, or speed of the object at the instant the thrower releases it, is the most important factor in the shot put. A fast projection speed will lead to a farther throw, because the shot put has a lot of forward momentum and will travel farther before gravity pulls it to the ground.

The turning technique was invented by American shot-putter Parry O'Brien in the 1950s. O'Brien stood at the back of the circle, facing opposite of the way he would ultimately face when flinging the shot. He then hopped backward on one leg and completed a half turn, pivoting his body while transferring his energy into shoving the shot. "It's an application of physics which says that the longer you apply pressure or force to an inanimate object, the farther it will go," O'Brien told *Time* when he was the magazine's cover story in December 1956 after winning Olympic gold in the shot put that year. "My style is geared to allow me to apply force for the longest time before releasing the shot."[23] Two decades later, American shot-putter Brian Oldfield improved on the O'Brien technique, using what is today the typical shot-put method. Standing at the back of the circle, the thrower starts an explosive spin, making almost two full turns within the circle before releasing the shot into the air. The added spinning movement gave Oldfield the edge to set a world record of 75 feet (23m) in 1975. It went unbroken for twelve years and is still one of the five longest shot-put throws ever recorded.

Gaining momentum by spinning the body in order to throw the shot put with a higher projection speed is essential to a good throw. The best shot-putters, however, also

Shot putter Parry O'Brien completes a throw under the watchful eye of officials during a competition in 1955. O'Brien developed a throwing technique that maximized the amount of time he applied force before making a shot.

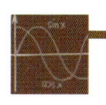

A Piece of the Pie

Throwing events involve physics, but good throwers must also understand math—especially geometry. The shot put, hammer, and discus all are thrown or flung from within a 7-to-8-foot circle (2.1m to 2.5m). Not only must the athlete's feet stay inside that circle at all times in order for the throw to qualify, he or she also must make the throw while standing within a specific sector, or section, of the circle. In geometry, a circle is made of 360 degrees of rotation. If a circle were divided into wedge-shaped slices, like a pizza, each slice would have a measurement smaller than 360 degrees. Each of these slices would be a sector, and all together, they would add up to 360 degrees. In throwing events, athletes must release each throw within a 35-degree sector, or slice, of the throwing circle to ensure that the object lands within a certain area of the field rather than flying off in any random direction. Field events could otherwise become dangerous for spectators. The rule that all throws be made within a precise sector of the circle further complicates the already difficult task of spinning to gain velocity for a throw.

must be aware of the angle at which they release the shot. Since it takes more force and energy for a heavy object to travel straight up in the air than horizontally, a shot thrown with too high of an upward angle wastes energy by being thrown *upward* instead of *outward*. If the thrower aims too low, however, energy gained during the spin will be used to drive the shot put even more rapidly toward the ground. Controlling the throwing angle while coming out of a dizzying spin is a difficult feat but one that is mastered by shot-putters who achieve the greatest distances, such as the current world record holders in the event: American Randy Barnes, who threw 23.12 meters, or about 76 feet, in 1990, and Russia's Natalya Lisovskaya, who set the women's record of 22.63 meters in 1987.

Hammer Time

Another field event is the hammer throw, and like the shot put, its history dates back many centuries. In the time of the Vikings men held throwing competitions using a stone attached to a wooden stick during religious festivals honoring Thor, the Norse god of thunder. The modern-day hammer throw no longer uses actual hammers, but rather a ball attached to a cable that has a handle at the other end. The men's ball weighs 16 pounds (7kg), and the women's weighs almost 9 pounds (4kg). As in the shot put, the thrower's feet cannot move outside a circle 7 feet (2.1m) in diameter, so to gain the projection speed that is necessary for a long-distance throw, the athlete spins in a circle.

An important difference between the shot put and the hammer throw is that the hammer is extended at the end of the cable, a distance of 4 feet (1.2m) from the thrower's body. When energy is applied to an object, its natural tendency is

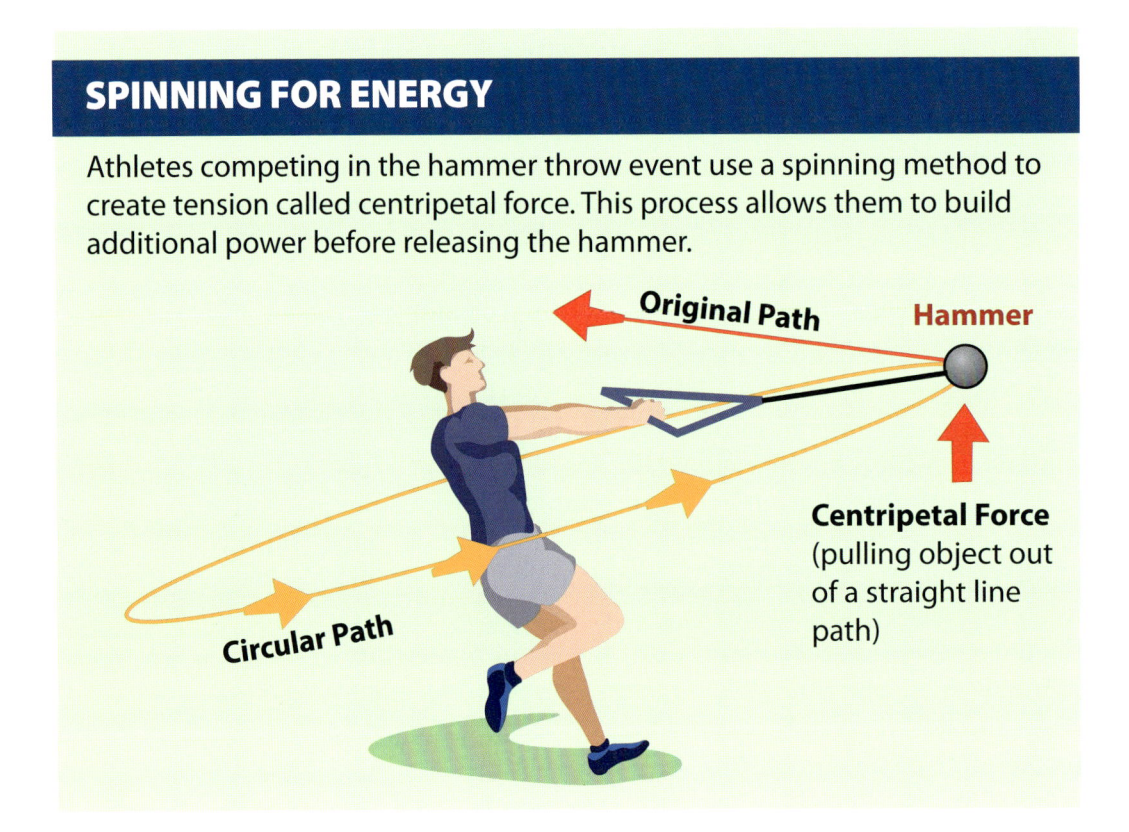

SPINNING FOR ENERGY

Athletes competing in the hammer throw event use a spinning method to create tension called centripetal force. This process allows them to build additional power before releasing the hammer.

Original Path

Hammer

Centripetal Force (pulling object out of a straight line path)

Circular Path

to travel forward in a straight line. Only if the object is constrained by something, such as the cable that tethers the hammer to the thrower during the spin phase of this event, will the object travel in a circle instead of a straight line. As the thrower spins at the center of the circle, therefore, the weight of the hammer pulls tight against the cable as it strives to overcome the spinning motion and instead move in a straight direction. The spinning process creates tension called centripetal force (the word *centripetal* comes from the Latin term for "center seeking"). The faster the thrower spins, the harder the hammer will pull against the cable in an effort to go straight. "The hammer throw is a rotary event that exerts a tremendous outward pull on the thrower," says former Olympian Gerry Carr. "This force increases from one rotation to the next as the athlete accelerates the hammer. The athlete must counteract this pull at all times."[24] When the athlete finally releases the handle after making three to four spins around the circle, the hammer follows its natural tendency to soar in a straight line, out and away from the throwing circle.

The ball used in the hammer throw and the shot used in the shot put are the same weight, but the distances achieved by the tethered spinning technique of the hammer throw are about four times greater. The men's world record in the hammer throw, set by Russian competitor Yuriy Sedykh in 1986, is 86.8 meters. The women's world record, set in 2010 by Anita Wlodaroczyk of Poland, is 78.3 meters. The difference in the record distances of the shot put and the hammer throw is due to centripetal force. Athletes who spin the hammer on the end of a cable while keeping their own footing and balance at the center of the throwing circle generate a great deal more energy to pass along to the hammer than do shot-putters who keep the shot close to their body at all times. The hammer, when the centripetal force placed on it is released, reaches higher velocity and flies much greater distances than the shot. (For this reason, the circle for the hammer throw is surrounded by a cage to prevent wayward hammers from flying out and injuring anyone.) The hammer throw, like the shot put, is a measure of brute strength, but also requires a unique understanding of the physical properties of momentum, energy, and inertia.

Making Hammer History

Every track-and-field event has its legendary competitors, and the hammer throw has Harold Connolly. His outstanding performance in the 1956 summer Olympics won him a gold medal. No American since has won gold in the hammer throw. Connolly also held the hammer throw world record for nine straight years, 1956–1965. But what made this legendary thrower stand out most was the fact that he succeeded despite a severe disability. At birth he weighed 12.5 pounds (5.7kg), an enormous size for a baby. Major nerves in his left shoulder were damaged during birth. As a result, Connolly grew up with a severely weakened left arm that he broke thirteen times as a child. When he reached adulthood, Connolly's left arm was 4 inches (10.1cm) too short and his left hand was considerably smaller than his right. Although he could not lift his left arm above his head, Connolly dominated the hammer throw event for the better part of a decade. After retiring from his four-time Olympic career, he became the director of U.S. programs for the Special Olympics, helping people with disabilities to compete in athletic events. Connolly died in August 2010 after having inspired millions during his lifetime.

Spin Doctors

In the shot put and the hammer throw, athletes try to overcome a heavy ball's natural tendency to fall quickly back to the earth due to gravity. Neither kind of throw is strongly affected by air resistance. Athletes who specialize in a third kind of throwing event, however, are keenly aware of the effects that the air moving around an object can have on its flight path and the distance it will travel. These athletes are discus throwers, and their event was one of the mainstays of the original Olympics in ancient times. "The concept of throwing a heavy, nondescript object such as a rock held no allure for the aesthetic-minded Greeks of the ancient Olympic era, who preferred the elegant lines of the discus,"[25] say Pagel and Pagel. Discus throwing is indeed an elegant event and one that involves intricate scientific details like aerodynamics, the science of how air moves around objects.

A discus is exactly what its name suggests—a disc. Its saucer-shaped surface is slightly thicker in the center of the circle and tapers out evenly toward its slimmer circumference, or outer edge. Men compete with a discus that weighs 4.4 pounds (2kg) and is 9 inches (22cm) in diameter—the distance from edge to edge of a circle, measured through its center point. Women use a 2.2-pound (1kg) discus that is 7 inches (18cm) in diameter. A discus is usually made from rubber, plastic, or aluminum with a metal core and a metal rim to add weight and keep the discus balanced evenly while airborne. The discus is also designed for spinning, which creates something called rotational inertia. Since inertia is the tendency of an object to resist changes in its position, rotational inertia is the tendency of a rotating, or spinning, object to resist changes in its position as it spins. Due to rotational inertia, an object spinning through the air tends to stay fairly level to the ground and has an even flight path,

With the discus gripped flat against the palm of his hand, a discus thrower looks to minimize air resistance and maximize rotational inertia by making a smooth throw during which the object stays flat.

A Toss-Up: Shot Put, Hammer Throw, Discus, and Javelin

LADIES FIRST

76.8 meters

The women's world record in discus is 76.8m (252ft), set by Germany's Gabriele Reinsch in 1988. This is the only track-and-field event in which the women's record exceeds the men's (74.1m, or 243 feet). Women throw a lighter discus, though.

---

instead of tilting or bobbing side to side or forward and backward. This concept is important to making sure that a discus smoothly slices through the air instead of wobbling, which would increase air resistance against its broad, flat surfaces and make it drop sooner to the ground.

Giving the discus speed and spin requires the right buildup before the throw. As in the shot put and the hammer throw, a discus thrower must stand within a circle to make the throw. In the discus, the circle is slightly larger than a shot put circle, with a diameter of 8 feet (2.5m), but discus throwers also must spin within that circle to gain momentum and generate the energy that will give the discus its projection speed once it is released. The discus thrower "knows that he has just the diameter of the circle in which to accelerate the discus to the greatest launch speed he can muster," says physics professor John Eric Goff. "By taking one and a half turns before the throw, he accelerates the discus through a distance about three times the circle's diameter."[26] The thrower holds the discus flat against the palm of the hand, with just his fingertips curved around the edge. He extends his throwing arm, and after making almost two complete turns around the circle, he flings the discus off the index finger of the throwing hand to send it spinning into the air. Once airborne, a discus takes flight. Thrown properly with the right amount of rotational inertia, or spin, it literally floats on the air, its aerodynamic properties helping it to stay aloft and fight gravity.

The discus's aerodynamic secret is in its shape. Its edges all slope evenly toward the center, so as it travels through the air, it is basically slicing the air. Air has mass, and this mass moves over and under the surface of the moving discus. If the thrower releases the discus with just the right upward tilt, air will "catch" against the underside, forcing the discus to shift away from the air in an upward direction. It is the same idea as the design of an airplane wing—the wing is shaped so that when the plane reaches a high takeoff speed, air moves under the wing in a pattern that lifts the plane. Similarly, when a discus thrower gives the disc enough initial speed and the right amount of spin to keep it from wobbling during takeoff the discus achieves lift, making a high arc in the air and traveling a long distance before gravity eventually pulls it back down.

A unique fact about a discus is that it can actually travel farther on a windy day. Throwing most objects into a headwind would slow them down in the face of greater air resistance and result in a shorter flight, but because of the discus's aerodynamic shape, greater air speed generated from wind force can drive the discus even higher into the air. The more height it can obtain before gravity inevitably pulls it back down toward Earth, the farther the distance of the throw will usually be. On windy days skilled discus throwers who know how to release the discus at the perfect angle and with the right amount of spin can achieve even greater throwing distances than on calm days. "It is common knowledge among throwers that a discus travels farther when it is spun at release and launched (like a glider) at an appropriate angle into a headwind," says engineering and biomechanics professor Brendan Burkett. "Discus throwers quickly learn which venues have winds that blow regularly from a favorable direction. They then try to compete at such venues as often as possible."[27] German thrower Jürgen Schult, for example, set the men's world discus record of 74.1 meters in 1986—reportedly on a very windy day.

Spearheading a Throw

A fourth type of throwing event depends, like the discus, on aerodynamics as much as on the strength and technique of the thrower. This event is the javelin, and it involves throwing a spear-shaped object out and away from the body. Like the discus, the javelin has a long ancestry dating back to ancient Greece. Perhaps more than any other track-and-field event, the javelin resembles an ancient military training exercise, since spears were a common weapon for soldiers in those days. Today's javelins are designed for sport, not battle,

ONE POWERFUL PITCH

A javelin thrower transfers his kinetic energy into the javelin itself through a process of three important phases.

1 Phase One:
The thrower sprints to gather energy. Before the foul line, he plants his feet to abruptly stop his legs from moving. This pushes the energy from his lower body upward into his torso.

2 Phase Two:
Energy from the legs and the torso is channeled into the athlete's throwing arm.

3 Phase Three:
This energy then passes into the javelin itself, which the runner releases in the third phase of the throw, using an overhand pitching style accomplished by rotating the shoulder, elbow, and wrist.

but the technique of throwing one still takes a great deal of strength, athleticism, and skill.

As in all throwing events, the projection speed of the object at the moment the thrower releases it is the biggest factor in determining the distance of the throw. The javelin is different from other throwing events, however, in that athletes are allowed to run to gain speed. Holding the javelin in one hand at shoulder height, the thrower sprints down a runway to gain as much velocity as possible. Since most of that velocity is in the runner's moving body, she must transfer her moving energy into the javelin itself. The process happens in three phases. First, the thrower sprints to accelerate her entire body. As she approaches the foul line, a point on the runway that throwers cannot cross, she plants her feet to abruptly stop her legs from moving. This pushes the energy from her lower body upward into her torso. Energy from the legs and the torso, both of which have now abruptly stopped moving, is then channeled into the athlete's throwing arm. The total velocity from the runner's body gets passed into the javelin itself, which the runner releases in the third phase of the throw, using an overhand pitching style accomplished by rotating the shoulder, elbow, and wrist.

"Of all throwing events," says Carr, "the javelin event most closely resembles the action of throwing a ball."[28] However, throwing a javelin is more challenging than pitching a ball. "Instead of winding up and throwing down off a mound, like a [baseball] pitcher does, you're running and throwing up into the air," says javelin coach Don Babbitt. "And you're sprinting at top speed, then planting on a hard surface that doesn't give. It's very stressful on the body."[29]

Once the thrower's pitching form sends the javelin airborne, the object depends on its aerodynamic properties to stay aloft. A javelin is essentially a long stick with a pointed front end, measuring at least 8.5 feet (2.6m) for men and 7.2 feet (2.2m) for women. The pointed end of the javelin is naturally aerodynamic, designed to slice through the air. The rest of the stick, however, is very prone to air resistance. If the angle of the throw is too high, the javelin could shift to a vertical position, exposing the full length of its surface to air resistance and halting any forward motion. Similarly, if the javelin begins to wobble up and down or from side to side, air will be hitting it all along its length, greatly slowing its speed and shortening its flight.

To counteract these potential problems, javelin throwers use spin, much the same way discus throwers do. By spinning the javelin in a clockwise motion at the instant she releases it (or a counterclockwise motion, if the thrower is left-handed), the athlete creates rotational inertia, which makes the javelin resist up-and-down or side-to-side changes in position. The spin gives the javelin a smooth flight and keeps it from wobbling, helping javelin throwers achieve the farthest distances of any throwing event in track and field. Three-time Olympic gold medalist Jan Zelezny of the Czech Republic set the men's world record in javelin at 323 feet (98.5m) in 1996, and his fellow countrywoman Barbora Spotakova has held the women's record of 237 feet (72.3m) since 2008.

Tossing and Turning

The incredible distances to which athletes are able to propel lead balls, flat discs, and spear-shaped poles demonstrate extraordinary strength, determination, and commitment to mastering the physical properties and behaviors of the objects they throw. Like the runners and jumpers who share the track and the field, throwers constantly strive to excel at a difficult task, beat their own former record, and vie for the title of the world's best. Throwers, perhaps more than any other track-and-field athletes, showcase both the strength and the ingenuity of the human spirit in athletic competition. They also stand out as examples of the physical accomplishments that are possible when an athlete commits to achieving personal fitness at the highest possible level.

CHAPTER **5**

Staying on Track: Fitness and Injury Prevention

Achieving personal excellence, whether in throwing, jumping, or running, means pursuing top physical fitness while avoiding injuries. A track-and-field team consists of many individuals who all specialize in particular events, often competing at different times and locations rather than in one simultaneous game or match. This makes their most common injuries different from those that many other kinds of athletes face. In contact sports like football or soccer, which require frequent physical confrontations among athletes, acute injuries are common. These are injuries that happen instantly from falling down, moving the wrong way, or colliding with another player, and they can be serious and traumatic events such as broken bones, wrenched joints, or head injuries. Track and field, on the other hand, is a noncontact sport. In its many different events, athletes at no time come into contact with one another, so there are far fewer opportunities for most track-and-field athletes to suffer things like broken bones or head injuries.

This does not mean that the track and the field are injury-free arenas. Any time people push their bodies to the very extremes of human ability, which happens every day in track-and field-events, injuries are a very real threat. Unfortunately, athletes training to compete at the highest possible level often pay no attention to the early signs of problems that could later become serious. "These athletes will push themselves to physical and psychological limits in order to achieve the ultimate goal, for some an Olympic gold medal or world record," say sports physicians Tom Adler, Phil Batty, Phillip Bell, and Bryan English. "They are therefore a very motivated breed with a tendency to overtrain and ignore 'niggly' injuries unless the coach and/or medical team can directly intervene."[30] Track-and-field athletes must find a balance between training enough to keep up with the competition and training too much, since the latter extreme can result in injuries.

Stressed-Out Bones

The human body consists of many different organ systems, or groups of organs, that work together to carry out essential functions. The system most central to track-and-field athletes is the musculoskeletal system, made up of the body's muscles, bones, and the tendons and ligaments that hold these parts together at joints. The bones of the arms and legs are known as long bones and are mainly responsible for helping the athlete to move. Therefore, they have a close relationship with the body's muscles, the powerhouse organs that give the body its energy and ability to do physical tasks. The muscles are attached to the bones by tough, fibrous tissue called tendons. At the joints, where two bones come together like in the knee or the elbow, both bones are connected by another type of tissue, called a ligament. The musculoskeletal system, with its muscles, bones, tendons, and ligaments, is responsible for allowing the body to do all physical things like run, jump, and throw. Track-and-field athletes, therefore, rely a great deal on these body parts, using them countless times every day. Unfortunately, this

MUSCLE MIGHT

6–7 meters
Average distance covered in a single second by a world-class sprinter running at top speed.

often leads to a common type of track-and-field ailment—a chronic injury, one that can occur over a period of time from constant use of the same body parts in the same repetitive motion.

One common chronic injury among runners afflicts the bones. Broken bones, at least in the sense that most people think of them, occur rarely in track and field. Bone fractures usually result from a sudden, strong impact that crushes or splits a bone, and this happens very infrequently among runners, jumpers, or throwers. A broken bone does not have to be caused by a sudden, traumatic injury, however. It can also be just a tiny crack in a bone, and such cracks often happen in the hip, lower leg, or foot bones of track-and-field athletes, especially those who run long distances day after day. This kind of crack is called a stress fracture, because it occurs from the stress put on the bone by thousands of footfalls. Runners suffering from stress fractures may not even realize that they have a broken bone. They may think the pain is simply due to overworked muscles or joints and will go away on its own in a day or two. Even though a stress fracture is just a slight crack, however, it will cause increasing pain if it is ignored. Stress fractures take time to heal, and are therefore one of the injuries that runners—especially those who run for distance—dread most. "Every runner fears a stress fracture," says Rob Rinaldi, a podiatrist who specializes in foot injuries. "Suspicion of a stress fracture ... begins with the athlete recognizing the earliest symptom: localized increased and unrelenting pain with exercise."[31] Left untreated, he says, this pain can become disabling, affecting the runner's performance.

All Torn Up

If distance runners worry about strain on their bones, sprinters worry about damage to their muscles. Sprinting puts an entirely different kind of strain on the lower body than distance running does. The act of building up to extreme speed from a standstill requires the muscles to work extremely hard, pivoting the leg bones powerfully

COMMON RUNNING INJURIES

Common track injuries, such as bone fractures and muscle strain, are often due to the chronic stress placed on the athlete's musculoskeletal system.

Stress fractures of the tibia and fibula bones

- Strained hamstring
- Iliotibial band syndrome, or ITBS
- Achilles tendonitis
- Plantar fasciitis
- Knee pain
- Stress fractures in the foot
- Calf muscle pulls
- Shin splints

where they meet at the joints. A sprinter's leg muscles are the most vulnerable parts of his body. From the instant he blasts out of the starting blocks at the beginning of the race, he places intense strain on his legs, and sometimes, this strain proves to be more than the muscles can withstand. Muscle tissue is made up of clumps of fibers that can stretch or even tear under extreme strain. A damaged leg muscle is a very painful injury that can impair a person's ability to run or even to walk. If this kind of injury happens

66 Track and Field

in the middle of a race, a sprinter will almost certainly lose, and may not even be able to make it to the finish line.

The most common injury among sprinters is a strained hamstring, the large muscle that runs along the back of the thigh. When sprinters surge their leg forward with each stride and grip the track with their foot, they then pull back hard on the grounded leg to drive the body forward. The muscle that does most of the pulling is the hamstring, and this is also the most likely muscle to suffer damage during an all-out sprint such as the 100-meter dash. "Hamstring [strain] is by far the most common injury in 100m sprinters, accounting for two-thirds of all injuries in this event," says sports physician John Orchard. "In maximal speed sprinting, the hamstring muscle group is the tissue closest to its injury threshold … hamstring strains are always going to be a common injury."[32]

SKINNY, BUT SPEEDY

The ideal body weight for long-distance runners is generally about 10 percent less than what is considered normal weight for a person's given height.

Throwing in the Towel

Throwers, too, are susceptible to muscle injuries if they strain especially hard during a particular performance. They can also experience injuries related to chronic use of their bodies during thousands of repetitive movements during practice. Unlike runners, throwers are equally vulnerable to injuries of their upper body *and* lower body, because they use their arms and shoulders as much as their legs.

All throwing events put strain on the joints, especially the shoulders and the elbows, but the hammer throw and the javelin are particularly stressful on a thrower's lower body too. In the hammer throw, the act of spinning the hammer around while using the body to pull against its hard spinning motion puts a great deal of strain on the knees, shoulders, and back. Javelin throwers, meanwhile, put tremendous tension on their entire body with each throw, especially on the knee and the elbow. "Elbow injuries tend to result from the forceful extension, and in some cases

A decathlon competitor grabs his elbow after making a throw in the javelin event. The forceful extension of the elbow when the javelin is released can result in injury.

Whatta-Gal Didrikson

The team that won the women's American Athletic Union national track-and-field championship in 1932 had only one member—a sporting phenomenon who competed in eight of the ten events, won five of them, tied for first place in a sixth, and set three world records during a single day of competition. Her name was Babe Didrikson.

Didrikson was a fierce competitor, but she lived in an era when women had limited opportunities in sports. For example, they could not compete in more than three events during a single Olympic tournament. Didrikson chose the 80-meter hurdles, the javelin throw, and the high jump. She won gold medals and set world records in the first two events and tied a world record in the high jump, but had to settle for a silver medal when her final jump was disqualified.

Babe Didrikson makes her gold medal-winning javelin throw at the 1932 Olympic Games in Los Angeles, California.

Surprisingly, track and field was not even the sport Didrikson loved best. Following the 1932 Olympics she took up golf, a sport she dominated for years. Didrikson died of cancer in 1956 at age forty-five, but not before showing the world that women deserved respect in sports. ESPN named Babe Didrikson the tenth best athlete (male or female) of the twentieth century.

hyperextension, of the elbow as the javelin is released," say sports injury experts Stephen Bird, Neil Black, and Philip Newton. "The knee is prone to injury because of the strain placed upon it as the thrower attempts to stop before the throwing line."[33] They add that throwing the javelin can injure the back and the throwing shoulder as well. Javelin throwers are among the track-and-field athletes most vulnerable to injury.

Heights of Danger

Jumping events are not without physical hazards, either. Because they begin each jump with a sprint, long jumpers and triple jumpers are at risk for the same kinds of muscle injuries that commonly afflict sprinters. The high jump, meanwhile, requires proper landing technique to avoid potentially serious injury to the head and neck. Most high jumpers land their jumps on the upper part of the shoulders. Landing incorrectly can put a great deal of strain on the neck, even so much as to break it.

A pole vaulter completes a successful jump with a safe, cushioned landing. A mistake during a jump can result in a fall that causes injury or death.

The pole vault is even riskier, since athletes must land their jumps from heights of up to 20 feet (6.1m) in the air. A flubbed jumping technique, especially in the first half of the jump when the athlete's body turns upside down on the way to clearing the crossbar, can mean plummeting to a bone-crushing fall. Unlike other events in which injuries can cause the athlete to lose the competition or even to miss out on a season, pole-vault injuries have the potential to be life threatening. Since 1980 forty-four American pole-vaulters of various ages have suffered catastrophic accidents, and twenty-eight of those have died, making the pole vault the most deadly sporting event in the United States. The most serious threat for pole-vaulters is a head injury from missing the landing mat and striking their head on the ground. Experts disagree about how to make the event safer, however. Helmets are one possible solution, although some athletes and coaches point out that a helmet would only transfer impact from a hard landing into the neck, which could be just as catastrophic. In spite of the dangers, pole-vaulters continue to pursue the sport they love, understanding that they undertake it at their own risk and must always train responsibly. "There's an element of risk in everything we do," says Jill Starkey, who qualified for the Olympic pole-vault trials in 2000. "It's hard for me to knock my own sport—it's a great, great event—but it has to be done right."[34]

Staying a Stride Ahead of Injuries

Track-and-field athletes practice for countless hours to perfect their techniques in the hope of avoiding overstraining and injuring themselves during competition. Sprinters run drill after drill, training their muscles to respond to important details such as the precise distance between their feet and the angle of their body in the starting blocks. Hurdlers practice until they know exactly how many steps to take in between hurdles during their race, making their event almost like an orchestrated dance; skipping a step would throw off their rhythm, which could make them stumble over a hurdle, hurt themselves, and lose their race. Jumpers, similarly, practice their approach technique until it becomes second nature.

They know exactly where on the runway to start the approach (this often differs from athlete to athlete based on their running style and the length of their legs). They also know how many steps they will take before the moment of the leap, and even where their launching foot should land at the moment of takeoff. Throwers also spend considerable time perfecting their approach, since a poorly performed throw could both disqualify the athlete and result in an injury.

Success at track and field involves more than just great technique, however. Athletes also train hard to develop whole-body fitness that can withstand the demands of intense competition. Many injuries, such as those to muscles, are more likely to happen if the body is not fit, since the athlete may try to compensate for weak or tired muscles by overusing other muscles or moving in a way that puts extra strain on the joints. Muscle strength is not the only measure of physical fitness, either. All track-and-field athletes need endurance, too—the ability to keep performing at a high level even when the body starts to feel tired. The best competitors in any event tend to be those who not only have powerful muscles but great endurance. Winning sprinters, for example, often have to compete in more than one race, since in a large meet races are run in heats, and the winners of each heat meet again for a final race to determine the overall champion. In events like the high jump and the pole vault, the best jumpers continue on to further rounds and higher heights until only one jumper remains as the victor. The best high jumpers and pole-vaulters, then, need the endurance to keep jumping higher and higher to remain in the competition.

All track-and-field athletes train for strength and endurance, but each event requires different kinds of training exercises because each uses different muscles in different ways. Throwers lift heavy weights to build stronger, more powerful muscles, especially in their upper body, and to get used to handling and maneuvering heavy objects. Sprinters, in addition to running repeated sprint sessions called intervals, also lift heavy weights to build and develop the large muscles and fast-twitch muscle fibers that give them explosive strength. Distance runners develop their muscles

A sprinter lifts weights under the direction of a trainer in order to improve her overall fitness level, which will improve her endurance and lower her risk of injury.

in different ways, avoiding lifting heavy weights in favor of exercises like leg lunges with light weights or workouts with stretchy devices called resistance bands. Such exercises build longer, leaner muscles filled with slow-twitch muscle fibers that conserve ATP's (adenosine triphospate's) fuel. Jumpers, meanwhile, often work on strengthening their core muscles—those of the abdomen, the hips, and the back—with exercises like abdominal crunches, leg lifts, and side bends.

No matter what event they compete in, track-and-field athletes are, as a group, some of the most physically fit

Staying on Track: Fitness and Injury Prevention 73

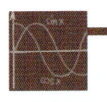

Eating to Win

Behind every winning track-and-field performance is a well-nourished and well-hydrated body. Runners, jumpers, and throwers need healthy diets with the right mix of carbohydrates, protein, iron, and vitamins to help their bodies build muscle, develop endurance, and function their best on race day. Carbohydrates are the mainstay of any track-and-field competitor's diet, since they are the nutrient the body's muscle cells break down to create ATP, adenosine triphosphate. Carbohydrates are found in breads, pasta, rice, fruits, and vegetables, which usually make up the bulk of a track-and-field athlete's diet. Protein from meat, nuts, and dairy products is important too, especially for sprinters and throwers trying to build muscle mass. Iron-rich foods are fundamental as well, because iron is the body's oxygen carrier in the bloodstream. Having too little iron in the body means the blood cannot carry as much oxygen to the muscles, making a runner feel sluggish and exhausted. Water, though, may be the most important requirement of all. Poor hydration, or having too little water in the body, has a negative effect on everything from muscle performance to mental focus and concentration. Athletes serious about performing to their best ability must start first with good nutrition and hydration.

people in the world. Through intense exercise regimens, they shape and hone their bodies to achieve extraordinary performances at a variety of challenging physical feats. The more fit they are, the better they will perform. Unfortunately, in their never-ending quest to best the competition, some track-and-field athletes have taken their extreme training tactics a little too far.

Chemical Enhancement

There are limits to how fast or how far people can run, how high they can jump, and what distance they can throw. There are limits, too, to how much muscle a person's body can develop. Track-and-field athletes are accustomed to pushing those limits, trying endlessly to best their own times, outperform their competitors, and topple world records. Their efforts to be the best have tempted many athletes in this sport to seek ways to enhance their own performance beyond what would be possible with strength and endurance training alone. Some turn to steroids.

Steroids are synthetic, or man-made, versions of the male sex hormone testosterone. This hormone is responsible for certain male gender characteristics, such as the growth of facial hair and the deepening of one's voice. It also helps to build lean muscle mass, and this is what tempts athletes to take steroids in an effort to boost their body's testosterone content. Steroid use can give athletes an edge in training,

Sprinter Marion Jones displays one of the five medals she won at the 2000 Olympic Games in Sydney, Australia. Jones was later stripped of her medals for using performance-enhancing drugs.

Staying on Track: Fitness and Injury Prevention

THE DIRT ON DOPING

20 percent

Approximate percentage of professional track-and-field athletes that are thought to use performance-enhancing drugs. This rate is second only to American football, in which an estimated 29 percent of professional players use them.

allowing them to work out harder and longer and build more muscle, strength, and endurance. For this reason, steroid use has become a persistent and growing problem among track-and-field athletes around the world. Runners, jumpers, and throwers who are posting record times and distances may be doing so with the help of steroids. Not wanting to lose to competitors they suspect are using performance-enhancing drugs, athletes are strongly tempted to use steroids too, in an effort to level the playing field. "I know six sprinters who tested positive [for steroids] in Seoul," says Canadian Ben Johnson, who set the world record in the 100-meter race at the 1988 Olympics in Seoul, South Korea, before being stripped of his gold medal for using steroids. "Some were in my final, some were in the 200m.... If they [Olympic officials] banned everybody who tested positive, they would ruin their industry."[35]

Athletes like Johnson have attempted to justify their use of steroids by pointing out that many other athletes use them, too. Unfortunately, steroid use is illegal for all track-and-field athletes, in part because it can do irreversible damage to the body. Steroid chemicals, which are either swallowed or taken by injection into the bloodstream, attach to the body's cells to change certain functions or behaviors of the body. When an athlete takes more of a steroid than the body can use, the extra, unused chemicals move to organs like the liver, the breasts, and the skin, where they begin to do damage. Steroids can cause men to develop female breast tissue, for example, and can shrink normal breast tissue in women. Steroids can cause acne, or tiny, pus-filled infections in the pores of the skin. They can give male traits to women, such as facial hair and a deep voice. They can affect the male sex organs, making some men sterile, or unable to produce sperm to father children. Most importantly, steroids can cause problems with the heart, the lungs, and the liver. Such damage may be life threatening and is often irreversible even if the person stops using steroids. In fact, the user may be unaware of this permanent damage until long after he or she stops using steroids. "Unlike almost all other drugs, all steroid based hormones have one unique characteristic," says Dr. Gary Wadler, a consultant to the U.S. Department of Justice on steroid use. "Their dangers may not manifest for months, years and even decades. Therefore, long after you gave them up you may develop side effects."[36]

Steroid use is not only dangerous, it also amounts to cheating. Some coaches have estimated that using steroids may give a sprinter up to a meter's worth of extra power in a race, for instance, which is enough for a win. Athletes who achieve outstanding performances may only do so because they have used steroids, whereas athletes who are "clean"—those who do not use steroids—may lose a competition because they lack that chemical edge. The organizations that oversee track-and-field competitions, such as the International Olympic Committee (IOC) and the International Association of Athletics Federations (IAAF)—the world governing body for track and field—are strongly opposed to the use of steroids. Professional athletes are tested for drug use after every competition, and if any traces of known steroids are found in their system, they may be punished by being stripped of any medals they won in the competition and getting banned from further competitions.

Even with these harsh punishments, however, many track-and-field athletes continue to use steroids. Some use the drugs during training and stop taking them before major competitions, in the hope that traces of the drug will be out of their system by the time they are tested. Others turn to new forms of steroids that drug tests do not yet recognize. Such was the case for American sprinter Marion Jones, who won three gold medals and two bronze medals in the 2000 summer Olympics in Sydney, Australia. Once considered the world's fastest woman and the greatest female athlete in the world, Jones fell from grace when investigators discovered she had used a powerful steroid, tetrahydrogestrinone (THG), also known as "the clear" because drug tests at that time could not detect it. Jones was stripped of her Olympic medals and served time in prison because she lied to federal investigators about using performance-enhancing drugs.

Even the downfall of superstars like Marion Jones as a result of steroid use has not deterred many track-and-field athletes from using such drugs. They simply seek out new versions that are not yet detectable. "Testing for drugs has become ever more prevalent," says author and historian Jan Stradling, "but with every new test comes the introduction of a new drug on the market or a new way to conceal it."[37] Many world-class track-and-field athletes have the idea that everyone else is already using a performance-enhancing drug, so by not using one themselves, they fear they are at a disadvantage. They often feel they are making a choice to "use or lose." And as soon as an athlete shows real promise on the track or in the field, the pressure to win becomes so intense that athletes may begin to feel losing is simply not an option.

CHAPTER 6

Ninety Percent Mental: The Psychology of Track and Field

Whether an athlete is a runner, a jumper, or a thrower, pressure to excel can be layered on by teammates, coaches, parents, fans, and especially the athlete himself. The sport of track and field is not about just keeping up with the competition, but outrunning or outdistancing everyone else. With the exception of relay races, in which each of four sprinters runs one-fourth of the total race distance, every event in track and field is a contest between individuals, and an outstanding performance by a single athlete will be noticed and remembered by the crowd—as could a heartbreaking loss. In track-and-field events, all the glory goes to the winner, and the runners-up may walk away feeling they are only second best. Success or failure at each event cannot be equally shared by the team, the way responsibility for a win or a loss can be shared by all team members in a sport like basketball or baseball. Instead, athletes in track and field tend to take their events very seriously and their losses very personally, and this can place them under heavy emotional stress leading up to an important competition.

Not only are these athletes encouraged to excel by the people around them and by their self-motivation, they are often tempted by cash as well. Since the 1970s, when track and field became a professional sport and not one just for amateurs, good athletes have been able to earn money for their performances. Some track-and-field meets offer cash prizes to winners, and many companies, like athletic clothing and equipment manufacturers Nike and Adidas, pay athletes to promote their products. Sponsors pay the athlete for such things as appearing in advertisements or speaking at events. The best athletes get the wealthiest and most famous sponsors, so athletic performance is about much more than the glory of winning a race, setting a world record, or earning a gold medal. It is also about making a living. Even athletes who are not yet professionals can be tempted by money. High school track-and-field athletes, for example, can be offered college scholarships if they excel at their events. At all levels of competition, the potential rewards for doing well in track and field (and the potential to miss out on those rewards for doing poorly) can add tremendously to the pressure an athlete feels when stepping up to the starting, throwing, or jumping line.

Once an athlete reaches a certain level of competition, such as a state or national championship meet, he or she knows that competitors have been training equally hard. All the athletes are in excellent physical shape. Often what will set the best competitors apart and allow one athlete to beat all others comes down to his or her mindset—the ability to tune out distractions and believe that it is possible to win. In track and field, the winning competitors are usually those who can excel under pressure, mentally fight off the feeling of fatigue, and even intimidate their fellow competitors with perfectly executed displays of athletic excellence in their quest for first place.

A Jungle of Jitters

Studying what goes on in the minds of athletes before, during, and after a competition is the job of sports psychologists. Psychology is the scientific study of the human mind

An athlete who experiences pre-competition anxiety (PCA) can struggle to perform at his best.

and its functions, especially the functions that affect behavior in certain situations. Sports psychologists study athletes' thoughts and feelings during practices and competitions. When thoughts have a negative effect on an athlete's performance, psychologists analyze why, and they try to help the athlete find ways to overcome the negativity.

Anxiety, or feelings of nervousness or unease about a coming event, is a psychological issue common to most

> ## HORSING AROUND
>
> Olympic sprinting legend Jesse Owens once defeated a racehorse in a 100-yard sprint (91m). (The horse, it is believed, had a slow start because it was frightened by the starting pistol.)

track-and-field athletes, and it is a serious problem for some. Nervous feelings before a major competition affect almost all track-and-field athletes to some degree. Called pre-competition anxiety, or PCA, these feelings can cause both mental and physical problems. Common symptoms of PCA are shaking or trembling, dry mouth, and nausea. Some athletes even vomit in the hours leading up to their event. PCA can also cause strong feelings of worry, nervousness, and dwelling on the possibility that things will go wrong during the competition. Anxiety also can cause sleeplessness, which in turn makes the athlete miss out on important rest her body needs the night before a competition.

PCA affects most athletes. "Standing on the starting line, we are all cowards,"[38] long-distance running champion Albert Salazar once said. Those who suffer from the strongest cases of PCA, however, may not perform as well during competitions as they do during practices. "For sports requiring endurance, power, or both," say sports psychologists Charles Hardy and Kelly Grace, "PCA can be very draining on an athlete's energy level."[39] In running events, this loss of energy can be a significant setback. Even for jumping and throwing events, PCA has the potential to ruin a performance. Track-and-field events such as the triple jump, high jump, javelin, discus, and shot put all require careful control of the muscles, and the tension felt when anxious can cause an athlete to perform poorly. "A high state of physical arousal can ... interfere with sports requiring a focused channeling of power," say Hardy and Grace. "Effective performances in these sports require some muscles to be tense and others to be relaxed. . . . Increased tension usually interferes with this channeling."[40]

Yet another effect of PCA is its tendency to make athletes dwell on everything that might occur in a competition. "These thoughts may be negative and result in preoccupation with what you can't do, rather than what you can do,"[41] say Hardy and Grace. According to sports psychologist Marc Jones and colleagues, athletes see a difficult competition as either an exciting challenge to succeed or a sinister threat that they might fail. The threat mindset "arises from the perception that winning is all-important, failure is unacceptable but likely, and the outcome of the competition is a significant reflection on the worth of the athlete as a competitor and as a person,"[42] they say. Such a mindset makes anxiety even worse before a competition. Athletes who worry too much about failing may bring about physical symptoms of anxiety and may lose a competition because of them. Once this happens, it can make the athlete even more nervous before

Is It All in Their Genes?

Runners from east Africa—countries like Ethiopia and Kenya—have long dominated distance running events. These champion runners seem to have endless stores of energy and routinely trounce competitors from other parts of the world. Many theories exist to explain why east Africa produces so many dominant long-distance runners. Perhaps their ancestors have passed down genes for bodies that are honed for running—most of these athletes are naturally tall and lanky. There has also been speculation that lifestyle factors such as dietary habits and running to and from school create the perfect recipe for an ideal runner's body. Still other experts theorize that the east African edge is more psychological than anything. Athletes of other nationalities have grown up hearing that east African runners are the world's best. Competitors may expect to lose to east Africans, and therefore, without even realizing it, they may not really try to win. The east Africans, meanwhile, enter the race with extreme confidence in their reputation, feeling that they can't lose. Psychology, more than any other factor, may best explain the phenomenon. Whatever its cause, east African runners are a force to be reckoned with over long distances.

future competitions. PCA is a negative cycle that can keep athletes from ever competing at their best.

Although most competitors experience some anxiety before a competition, say Hardy and Grace, "Elite athletes channel this energy to work for them rather than against them."[43] The most successful track-and-field athletes are the ones who learn to see difficult competition as a challenge and not a threat. "There is less emphasis on the outcome of competitions and greater emphasis on athletes enjoying the process of the sport regardless of whether they win or lose,"[44] say Jones and colleagues. Top track-and-field athletes learn to be satisfied with giving their all, and therefore, they feel successful no matter the outcome of the race. "The medals don't mean anything and the glory doesn't last," says Jackie Joyner-Kersee, holder of the women's world record in the heptathlon (a seven-event combination of sprints, jumps, hurdles, and throws). "It's all about your happiness," she says. "The rewards are going to come, but the happiness is just loving the sport and having fun performing."[45] Joyner-Kersee's mindset seemed to help in her journey to becoming one of the greatest female athletes in history.

Playing Mind Games

The right mindset is essential to performing at one's physical best, and some athletes even use others' feelings of nervousness or insecurity to their own advantage. This is especially true in running events. Unlike jumps and throws, which involve only one competitor at a time, track races require runners to stand together on the starting line and compete against one another. Athletes in a running race do more than just focus on their own performance. They also analyze what their competition is doing at any given moment, and this can have a positive or a negative effect on the race.

The shorter a race, the less time there is to think about what the competition is doing. In the 100-meter dash, for example, which is over in a matter of seconds, it is essential for runners to focus on their own movements instead of getting distracted by the runners to their left or right. Nevertheless, sprinters are very aware of whether they are

A sprinter turns to keep an eye on his competition. Such movement can cost a sprinter precious milliseconds during a race.

winning the race or whether someone else is ahead of them. Either scenario can place psychological stress on the runner—if she is ahead of the competition, she may fear being passed by another runner before she can make it to the finish line. She might even look from side to side as she runs (a movement that, in a sprint, can cost the runner precious fractions of a second). If a sprinter realizes she is falling behind, however, she may feel discouraged or dismayed and may mentally give up and stop trying her best in the middle of the race. "If athletes see their goals as unattainable," says collegiate and Olympic sprinting coach Curtis Frye, "they will reduce their effort, thus reducing their chances for success." He says that being psychologically prepared to handle the stress of competition is as important as physical training. "Mental toughness allows . . . athletes to reach their goals."[46]

The longer the race, the more time there is for runners to dwell on their fear of getting passed or to feel defeated and discouraged. For this reason, long-distance races often become psychological battles as much as physical ones. As competitors complete lap after lap of the race, they carefully gauge their remaining stores of energy to decide how fast they need to run and how much energy to save for the finish. Unlike sprinters, distance runners often prefer to hold back, letting one or two competitors stay ahead of them for most of the race while planning to sprint at the end and overtake their rivals. Leading a long-distance race is not always an advantage, because the leader always fears that at the end a fast finisher will come up from behind and steal the win. Runners who hang back to keep their competitors ahead of them, however, must also prepare for the possibility that they will not be able to run fast enough at the end to overtake the lead runner. Distance runners play a complicated game of psychological warfare during their races, always trying to keep their competitors guessing as to who is feeling tired and who still has enough energy to charge past the others and win.

Bill Toomey, 1968 Olympic gold medalist in the decathlon (a competition featuring a mix of ten different running and field events), describes the importance of outsmarting the competition in endurance races. "It's like when a guy comes up to you and says before a race, 'Are you in shape?' I'm not going to tell him I'm not. I'll say I'm in the greatest shape of my life, and they will follow you right around the track."[47] The distance runner who can make his rivals believe he is tireless, even though he may feel tired, will often win. Long races show the importance of mental, not just physical, toughness in track and field.

Miracle Moments

Track-and-field athletes are always chasing someone or something. They either set their sights on beating a particular competitor or on chasing down a new record in their

Jonathan Edwards of Great Britain reacts in disbelief after becoming the first athlete to make a triple jump that surpassed a distance of 18 meters.

Ninety Percent Mental: The Psychology of Track and Field

event. Usually, a group of the "best" competitors rises to the top in a given level of competition, whether it is high school, college, professional, or Olympic. This same handful of competitors usually battles to place in the top three or four spots. They train physically and prepare themselves mentally for the stress of track-and-field competitions, and the winner often performs just a fraction of a second faster, jumps a few centimeters higher, or throws a couple inches farther than the others. Sometimes, however, an athlete annihilates competitors with a particularly outstanding performance that shatters records and leaves rivals, spectators, and sometimes even the athlete himself rubbing their eyes in disbelief. This was true for British triple jumper Jonathan Edwards in the 1995 track-and-field world championships, when he became the first athlete ever to surpass 18 meters in the triple jump. Edwards' startling leap cleared the yellow distance indicator set up along the edge of the pit by 0.16 meters. The indicator ended at 18 meters even, which was farther than anyone—until Edwards—was expected to be able to jump.

Such record-blasting performances are often one-time-only affairs, likened to the athlete's having an extraordinarily good day on the track or in the field (and sometimes spurring rumors that the athlete was using steroids, though this certainly is not always the case). The very athlete who sets the record may never perform that well again. This has long been a mystery among those who participate in or watch track and field. The athletes who post amazing times, heights, or distances are often as perplexed as everyone else and may be frustrated if they cannot recreate the performance a second time. It is possible that anxiety before a particularly stressful competition creates an especially strong surge of endorphins—pain-killing and nerve-calming molecules released by the cells of the body's nervous system during times of excitement or stress. Endorphins might improve the athlete's physical and mental well-being to the point where a record-shattering performance is possible, whereas the same athlete, when not faced with exactly the same combination of stress and excitement as she was on that day, will not be able to perform quite as well again.

Flo Jo's Mojo

She stepped onto the track in the 1988 Olympic tournament in Seoul, South Korea, with her long fingernails painted red, white, blue, and gold—the first three colors for her country, the fourth for the medals she was confident she would win in the 100-meter and 200-meter dashes. Not only did she win gold in both events, she also set world records that no other female runner has come close to breaking in the decades since. Florence Griffith-Joyner's name has long been that of the fastest woman in the world.

She was also one of track and field's most colorful characters. From humble beginnings in the projects of Los Angeles, Griffith-Joyner, also known by the nickname "Flo Jo," rose to stardom not just as a super athlete but an actress, writer, and spokesperson. She even became a fashion designer, creating her own flashy running outfits to wear in her charges toward the finish line. Charming, confident, and caring, Flo Jo was a role model to countless Americans. She died suddenly in her sleep in 1998 at age thirty-eight, perhaps due to a seizure—a sudden surge of electrical activity in the brain. Her legacy, however, lives on, and no woman has ever been known to run faster.

Florence Griffith-Joyner poses with the medals she won at the 1988 Olympic Games in Seoul, Korea.

There Are No Limits

Whether endorphins are responsible for an amazing performance or whether it is simply due to outstanding physical and mental fitness, those who watch, coach, or compete in track and field notice one unavoidable trend—athletes are always getting stronger, faster, and better, and there is seemingly no limit to how much they can accomplish. There was a time in history when it was thought impossible for a person

England's Roger Bannister reaches the finish line as the first man to run a mile in under four minutes at a race in 1954.

to run a mile in less than four minutes, but in 1954 English runner Roger Bannister broke the 4-minute mile, completing the distance in 3 minutes, 59 seconds. Now, milers beat the 4-minute mark all the time, pursuing the current world record of 3 minutes, 43 seconds set in 1999 by Moroccan runner Hicham El Guerrouj. It was once thought impossible for a sprinter to run 100 meters in less than 10 seconds, too. Nowadays, Usain Bolt's record of 9.58 seconds stands tall—until he or someone else comes along to break it. "We have to rethink everything we know about human performance," says Ato Boldon, four-time Olympic sprint medalist and NBC commentator, reacting to Bolt's jaw-dropping speed. "I used to talk about times in the area of 9-low [seconds] as some kind of unicorn-like fantasy, but he [Bolt] has made fantasy into reality."[48]

Jumpers, runners, and throwers are endlessly seeking to nudge the world record up, out, or down by just a bit more. Though many record holders' accomplishments stand for years or even decades, the world's best track-and-field athletes believe that records are made to be broken. Track and field, like no other sport in the world, tests the very boundaries of human performance. From the time of the ancient Greeks to today, athletes have not stopped improving. As yet, there are no clear limits to what the human body can do. In track and field, athletes survive on the certainty that anything is possible.

NOTES

Chapter 1: A Run Through Track-and-Field History

1. Nigel B. Crowther. *Sport in Ancient Times*. Westport, CT: Praeger, 2007, p. 61.
2. David C. Young. *A Brief History of the Olympic Games*. Malden, MA: Blackwell, 2004, p. 137.
3. Joseph M. Turrini. *The End of Amateurism in American Track and Field*. Urbana: University of Illinois Press, 2010, pp. 9–10.
4. Turrini. *End of Amateurism*, p. 10.
5. Vassil Girginov and Jim Parry. *The Olympic Games Explained: A Student Guide to the Evolution of the Modern Olympic Games*. New York: Routledge, 2005, p. 171.

Chapter 2: The Race Is On: Sprints, Distance Races, and Hurdles

6. Quoted in Philip Hersh. "Usain Bolt Smashes 100-Meter Record, Clocking a 9.58." *Chicago Tribune*, August 17, 2009. http://articles.chicagotribune.com/2009-08-17/news/0908160426_1_bolt-strikes-usain-bolt-tyson-gay.
7. Clyde Williams. "Physiological Demands of Sprinting and Multiple-Sprint Sports." In *The Olympic Textbook of Science in Sport*, edited by Ronald J. Maughan. Chichester, UK: John Wiley & Sons, 2009, pp. 29–30.
8. Henry K.A. Lakomy. "Physiology and Biochemistry of Sprinting." In *Handbook of Sports Medicine and Science: Running*, edited by John A. Hawley. Oxford, UK: Blackwell Science, 2000, p. 1.
9. Williams. "Physiological Demands of Sprinting," p. 31.
10. Williams. "Physiological Demands of Sprinting," p. 31.
11. Roy Benson. "Lite Weights." *Running Times*, April 2007, p. 23.
12. Ed Housewright. *Winning Track and Field for Girls*. 2nd ed. New York: Chelsea House, 2010, p. 80.
13. Housewright. *Winning Track and Field*, p. 80.
14. Gary Barber. *Getting Started in Track & Field Athletics*. Victoria, BC: Trafford, 2005, p. 83.

Chapter 3: Up, Up, and Away: Jumping Events and the Pole Vault

15. Housewright. *Winning Track and Field*, p. 80.
16. Arthur E. Chapman. *Biomechanical Analysis of Fundamental Human Movements*. Champaign, IL: Human Kinetics, 2008, p. 142.
17. Mark Guthrie. *Coaching Track and Field Successfully*. Champaign, IL: Human Kinetics, 2003, pp. 155–156.
18. Cliff Rovelto. "High Jump." In *Winning Jumps and Pole Vault*, edited by Ed Jacoby. Champaign, IL: Human Kinetics, 2009, p. 63.
19. Gerry Carr. *Fundamentals of Track and Field*. 2nd ed. Champaign, IL: Human Kinetics, 1999, p. x.
20. Chapman. *Biomechanical Analysis*, pp. 142–143.
21. Housewright. *Winning Track and Field*, pp. 80–81.

Chapter 4: A Toss-Up: Shot Put, Hammer Throw, Discus, and Javelin

22. Kent Pagel and Ramona Pagel. "Shot Put." In *Complete Book of Throws*, edited by L. Jay Silvester. Champaign, IL: Human Kinetics, 2003, p. 39.
23. Quoted in *Time*. "Sport: The Great White Whale." December 3, 1956. www.time.com/time/magazine/article/0,9171,808666-1,00.html.
24. Carr. *Fundamentals of Track and Field*, p. 261.
25. Pagel and Pagel. "Shot Put," p. 39.
26. John Eric Goff. *Gold Medal Physics: The Science of Sports*. Baltimore: Johns Hopkins University Press, 2010, p. 154.
27. Brendan Burkett. *Sport Mechanics for Coaches*. 3rd ed. Champaign, IL: Human Kinetics, 2010, p. 130.
28. Carr. *Fundamentals of Track and Field*, p. ix.
29. Quoted in Alan Grant. "Rogue Spear." *ESPN Magazine*, February 25, 2008. http://sports.espn.go.com/espnmag/story?id=3264219.

Chapter 5: Staying on Track: Fitness and Injury Prevention

30. Tom Adler, Phil Batty, Phillip Bell, and Bryan English. "Sports Specific Injuries." In *Essential Sports Medicine*, edited by Richard Higgins, Peter Brukner, and Bryan English. Malden, MA: Blackwell, 2006, p. 118.
31. Rob Rinaldi. "The Dreaded Stress Fracture." *Vermont Sports Magazine*, May 31, 2009. http://vtsports.com/the-dreaded-stress-fracture.
32. Quoted in "Muscle Injury in Sport." Physioroom.com. www.physioroom.com/experts/expertupdate/interview_john_orchard_20030928.php.
33. Stephen Bird, Neil Black, and Philip Newton. *Sports Injuries: Causes,*

Diagnosis, Treatment, and Prevention. Cheltenham, UK: Stanley-Thomas, 1997, p. 200.

34. Quoted in Dan McQuade. "Has Pole Vaulting Become Too Dangerous?." *Daily Pennsylvanian*, April 25, 2002. www.dailypennsylvanian.com/node/26605.
35. Quoted in Jeff Powell. "Ben Johnson Claims to Be the Victim of an American Conspiracy." *The Daily Mail*, May 30, 2008. www.dailymail.co.uk/sport/othersports/article-1023170/EXCLUSIVE-Ben-Johnson-reviled-drugs-cheat-history-claims-victim-American-conspiracy-Now-says-evidence-tape-Deluded-fantasist-whistleblower-decide.html.
36. Quoted in ESPN.com. "Anabolic Steroids." September 6, 2007. http://espn.go.com/special/s/drugsandsports/steroids.html.
37. Jan Stradling. *More than a Game: When Sport and History Collide*. Sydney: Pier 9, 2009, p. 279.

Chapter 6: Ninety Percent Mental: The Psychology of Track and Field

38. Quoted in Benjamin H. Cheever. "Finding My Stride." *Runner's World*, November 2007, p. 107.
39. Charles Hardy and Kelly Grace. "Dealing with Precompetitive Anxiety." *Sport Psychology Training Bulletin* vol. 1 (1996), p. 3,513.
40. Hardy and Grace. "Dealing with Precompetitive Anxiety," p. 3,513.
41. Hardy and Grace. "Dealing with Precompetitive Anxiety," p. 3,514.
42. Marc Jones, Jim Taylor, Miyako Tanaka-Oulevey, and Mary Grigson Daubert. "Emotions." In *Applying Sports Psychology: Four Perspectives*, edited by Jim Taylor and Gregory Scott Wilson. Champaign, IL: Human Kinetics, 2005, p. 73.
43. Hardy and Grace. "Dealing with Precompetitive Anxiety," p. 3,514.
44. Jones, Taylor, Tanaka-Oulevey, and Daubert. "Emotions," p. 73.
45. Quoted in Housewright. *Winning Track and Field*, p. 41.
46. Curtis Frye. "100 and 200 Meters." In *USA Track & Field Coaching Manual*, edited by Joseph L. Rogers. Champaign, IL: Human Kinetics, 2000, p. 49.
47. Quoted in Don Holst and Marcia S. Popp. *American Men of Olympic Track and Field: Interviews with Athletes and Coaches*. Jefferson, NC: McFarland, 2005, p. 135.
48. Quoted in Hersh. "Usain Bolt Smashes 100-Meter Record, Clocking a 9.58."

GLOSSARY

adenosine triphosphate (ATP): An energy-carrying molecule produced in the cells of all living things.

aerodynamics: The study of the properties of air movement and how air interacts with objects.

air resistance: A force created by air's mass as it pushes against a moving object.

center of gravity: The single point or location within an object where its total weight and mass are perfectly balanced.

centripetal force: The force necessary to keep an object moving in a curved path, because its natural tendency is to move in a straight line.

endorphins: Hormones released by the brain and nervous system that have a relaxing and pain-relieving effect on the body.

endurance: The ability to withstand hard physical activity or stress for long periods.

friction: The resistance created when one object or surface moves against another.

gravity: The force that attracts anything with mass to all other things that have mass.

inertia: The tendency of objects to stay still if at rest or to keep moving if in motion, unless they are acted on by an outside force.

kinetic energy: The energy of an object that is in motion.

mass: A measurement of how much matter (how many molecules) is in an object or a body of gas or liquid.

momentum: A measure of motion in a moving body, found by multiplying its mass by its velocity.

potential energy: Energy stored in an object because of its position.

projection speed: The speed of a thrown object at the instant the thrower releases it.

steroids: Man-made hormones, sometimes used by athletes to improve their athletic performance.

velocity: The speed of an object moving in a specific direction.

FOR MORE INFORMATION

Books

Gary Barber. *Getting Started in Track and Field Athletics: Advice & Ideas for Children, Parents, and Teachers.* Victoria, BC: Trafford, 2006. Gives rules and techniques for the various track-and-field events, plus tips on how new athletes can get started.

Ed Jacoby, ed. *Winning Jumps and Pole Vault.* Champaign, IL: Human Kinetics, 2009. Written by well-known track-and-field coaches; explains the biomechanics and training tactics of the long jump, triple jump, high jump, and pole vault.

Katie Marsico. *Real World Math: Sports—Running.* Ann Arbor, MI: Cherry Lake, 2008. Analyzes the relationship between math and the process of running.

Jim Parry and Vassil Girginov. *The Olympic Games Explained: A Student Guide to the Evolution of the Modern Olympic Games.* New York: Routledge, 2005. Introduces the history of the Olympic Games, from their Ancient Greek origins through today. Includes study tasks and review questions.

Luke Thompson. *Track and Field: Track Events.* New York: Children's, 2000. Gives an overview of various running events in track and field, including sprints, distance races, and hurdles.

Kristin Wolden Nitz. *Play by Play Field Events.* Minneapolis: Lerner, 2004. Explores all the jumping and throwing field events in track and field.

Articles

Dierdre Van Dyk. "How Fast Can Humans Go?" *Time.* August 22, 2008, www.time.com/time/health/article/0,8599,1835420,00.html. Investigates the reasons why champion sprinters are so fast and whether there are limits to human performance in running.

Websites

ESPN's Track and Field newswire (http://espn.go.com/espn/wire?sportId=1700). Provides constantly updated information on world track-and-field news, including the most recent wins and records around the world.

London 2012 (www.london2012.com/olympic-stadium). Official website of the 2012 summer Olympic Games in London; explores the science behind designing and building sporting surfaces for athletes in track and field and other Olympic sports.

Official Website of the Olympic Movement (www.olympic.org/). Has sections on the various Olympic sports, the athletes, the history of the Olympic Games, and a search feature for finding medalists in any event or year since the Olympics began.

Runner's World Kids' Running Guide (www.runnersworld.com/article/ 0,7120,s6-238-267--11828-0,00.html). Sponsored by *Runner's World* magazine, offers tips for junior athletes to get involved with running for fun and competition.

USA Track & Field, Athlete Bios (www .usatf.org/athletes/bios/). Biographies of all current and recent track-and-field athletes on the U.S. national team, plus biographies of hall-of-fame stars, maintained by the official website of USA Track & Field, Inc.

INDEX

A
Amateur Athletic Union of the United States (AAU), 14–15
Athlete, 13
ATP (adenosine triphosphate) molecules, 26–27, 29, 74

B
Bannister, Roger, 90, *90*
Barnes, Randy, 53
Bolt, Usain, 22, 91

C
Centripetal force, 54–55
Connolly, Harold, 56
Coubertin, Pierre de, 15–17

D
Didrikson, Babe, 69, *69*
Discobulus, "the discus thrower" (Myron), *11*
Discus thrower, *16*
Discus throwing, 56–59
Distance jumping, 38–40
Distance races
 distance variations, 28–29
 east African domination, 83
 muscle requirements, 28–29
 psychological and mental aspects, 86
 strides, 28–29
 technology of measurement, 33–34, *33*
 track dimensions and description, 30–32
 twitch, 29
Dragila, Stacy, 45

Drugs for performance improvement, 74–78

E
Edwards, Jonathan, *87*
Egypt, 9–10, *10*
El Gherrouj, Hicham, *28*, 90
Endorphins, 88, 89

F
Fantastic Four, 50
Fitness, 63–64
Fosbury, Dick, 42–43
Fosbury Flop, *43*

G
Garrett, Robert, *16*
Greece, 10–13
Griffith-Joyner, Florence (Flo Jo), 89, *89*

H
Hammer throw, 54–56
High altitude, 22
High jumping, 40–44, *41*
Horizontal jumping, 40
Hurdler, *30*
Hurdling, 30–31
Hydration, 74

I
Injuries, running, 65–67, *66*
International Association of Athletics Federations (IAAF), 76
International Olympic Committee (IOC), 76

J
Javelin throwing, 59–62, *61*
Johnson, Ben, 76
Jones, Marion, *75*, 77–78
Joyner-Kersee, Jackie, 84
Jumping events
    distance jumping, 38–40
    gravity, 35–39
    injuries, 70–71
    long jumping, *36*
    techniques, 37–38
    types and styles, 38–44
Junior Olympics, 10

L
Lewis, Carl, 37, 50
Lisovskaya, Natalya, 53

M
Marathon races, 17
Muscle energy loss, 27
Muscles and bones, 23–24
Musculoskeletal system, 64–65
Myron, 11

N
Newton, Isaac, 50
Nourishment, 74

O
O'Brien, Parry, 50, *52*
Oerter, Al, 50
Olympic Games
    ancient throwing, running and jumping events, 11–13
    current v. ancient, 18–19
    first modern games, 16–18
    first women pole vaulters, 45
    origins in ancient Greece, 11–13, *12*
    track and field popularization, 16–18
Overtraining, 63–64
Owens, Jesse, *37*, 82

P
Performance enhancement drugs, 74–78
Photo finish, 33
Physical requirements, 63–65
Pole vaulting, 44–47, *70*
Pre-competition anxiety (PCA), 81–84, *81*

R
Races, types of, 20, 22
Raising the bar, 39
Rosen, Mel, 22
Running
    air resistance, 26
    ATP (adenosine triphosphate) molecules, 26–27, 29
    challenges, 26–27
    curve navigation, 32–33
    differences in tracks, 22
    distance races, 28–30
    finish line timing technology, 33–34, *33*
    friction, 26–27
    ideal runner's weight, 67
    initial strides, 26
    injuries, 65–67, *66*
    muscle energy loss, 27
    muscles and bones, 23–24
    physical process, 24–25
    split second starts, 24

S
Schmidt, Jürgen, 59
Sedykh, Yuri, 55
Shot putting, 49–53, *49*
Sotomayor, Javier, *41*
Spotakova, Barbara, 62
Sprinting, 20, 22, 23–27, *23*, *25*, 84–85, *85*
Starkey, Jill, 71
Starting blocks, 25
Steroids, 75–78
Stress fractures, 65

T

Throwing events
- discus throwing, 56–59, *57*
- hammer throw, 54–56
- injuries, 67, *68*, 69
- mathematics involved, 53
- shot putting, 49–53, *49*

Toomey, Bill, 86

Track and field
- ancient Greece, 11–13
- arena, *21*
- athletic technique development, 71–73
- chemical performance enhancement, 74–78
- distance races, 28–30, *29*
- finish line, 33–34, *33*
- fitness training and practices, 72–74, *73*
- main divisions, 20
- in the modern world, 18–19, *18*
- moments of triumph, 86–89, *87*
- 19th century United States, 14–15, *14*
- psychological and mental aspects, 79–91
- record-breaking performances, 89–91, *90*
- *See also specific events*

Track differentials, 22
Track dimensions, 31–32
Track ovals, 32–33
Triple jumping, 39–40
Turning technique, 51, *52*, 53

W

Wlodaroczyk, Anita, 55

Z

Zelezny, Jan, 62

PICTURE CREDITS

Cover Photo: © Pete Saloutos/Shutterstock.com
© Ace Stock Limited/Alamy, 12
© Action Plus Sports Images/Alamy, 36
© Aspen Photo/Shutterstock.com, 46
AFP/Getty Images, 33
Andy Lyons/Allsport/Getty Images, 68
AP Images/Hans Deryk, 41
AP Images/Mark Baker, 85
© Charles Miller/Alamy, 9
Christian Petersen/Getty Images, 57
Clive Brunskill/Allsport/Getty Images, 87
Donald Miralle/Getty Images, 70
Gale, Cengage Learning, 21, 43, 54, 60, 66
George Silk/Time Life Pictures/Getty Images, 52
Getty Images, 69
Getty Images for Norwich Union, 73
Getty Images Sport/Getty Images, 16
© Gianni Dagli Orti/Corbis, 11
Gustoimages/Photo Researchers, Inc., 38
Hulton Archive/Getty Images, 37
© ImageState/Alamy, 30
Keystone/Getty Images, 90
Mark Dadswell/Getty Images, 49
Matthew Stockman/Allsport/Getty Images, 75
© PCN Photography/Alamy, 18
© Peter Bernik/Shutterstock.com, 25
© Stock Connection Blue/Alamy, 81
Stu Forster/Allsport/Getty Images, 28
Three Lions/Getty Images, 14
Tony Duffy/Getty Images Sport/Getty Images, 89
© View Stock/Alamy, 27
Wieslaw Smetek/Photo Researchers, Inc., 23

ABOUT THE AUTHOR

Jenny MacKay has written fourteen nonfiction books for middle-grade and teen readers. She lives with her husband, son, and daughter in northern Nevada, where she was born and raised. She ran long distance for track and field in high school and still likes to jog, but she shuns formal races nowadays because she suffers from severe pre-competition jitters.